COPYRIGHT
This book is solely published by the author, Brian Doherty.
reproduced, in part or in whole, without the written permis
author.

The views, conclusions and experiences reproduced in this book are purely those of the author and are based on his personal experiences during the fourteen and a half years he spent in various homes.

Acknowledgments

I would like to express my most heartfelt and grateful thanks to the following people for their undeniable help with compiling book.

Firstly, my thanks go out to Mr. Pat Magart, editor-in-chief of the Derry Journal, who gave me copyright permission to reproduce any stories and photographs reported in print from back issues of the Derry Journal.

Then, Ian Cullen, a reporter from the Derry Journal, who gave me the inspiration to compile my story.

David Bigger for his donation of photographs.

Mr.Brian Barr from the Guild hall, Derry, who gave me my first real insight into my early days through the midwives book.

The Sisters from the Mother House in Hammersmith, London.

Also, the Staff at The British Newspaper Library in Colindale for their patience with me.

*Not forgetting the one person in my life who has helped me, that is, my wife Barbara, whose patience never faltered. She has been with me all the way. Thank you
For being there for me whenever I needed a shoulder to lean on. Thank you.*

INTRODUCTION

THE 'SYSTEM'

In my view, in many instances, the fundamental duty of protecting the child from harm was violated. As children, we were the victims of cruel and very excessive punishment and other physical abuse.

Education was so limited or virtually non-existent that some children have progressed through their lives with minimal literacy skills. For many, this lack of education has placed them at a severe disadvantage in later years as far as employment and personal development.

As my home, Termonbacca, was run by a Catholic Religious Order, this ensured that we had a very heavy diet of religious instruction and a minimum of literacy skills. Once again, this has left a lot of us with a severe disadvantage in later life.

COULD YOU DREAM THIS NIGHTMARE ?

By Brian Doherty

The beginning for me. Brian Doherty ?

The following details I have discovered from official records and entries after much endless research and poring over old documents. Most people come from a loving mother who I dare say you have heard talking about all the details of your delivery and the ups and downs of her labour. Telling you what your first smile was like. How cute and lovable you were and how you cried for food after your wonderful birth. Most mothers take great joy in telling you these tales in your later life.

Not my mother as I found out at the age of fifty four, but from a dirty watermarked midwife's record book which had been discarded and thrown on a skip in Derry. Fortunately for me this was rescued and is now in Londonderry. It seems from the entry that I was born on a Monday in the Waterside Hospital, Derry in 1947. This hospital was previously a workhouse, cold, dark, damp and uncaring. The record states in black ink:-

1947
Baby Boy Brian Coleman Doherty - mother
(No mention of a father) **Breastfed - three weeks**

Three whole weeks and she could stand me no longer with four other children already. It was just ten days before Christmas with joy in the air and the festivities all around. It is as we all know the season of good will and giving.

Well this is what my mother did. She gave me away. No, not in the sense we all know of as joy and wrapping a present up with a pretty bow. She coldheartedly gave me up to an orphanage called, *'Fahan'*, in Donegal.

This was on 15.12.1947. I was there for three years. I only know this from record books. I do not remember anything of these first three years of my life.

In 1950 my nightmare began when I was transferred to St. Joseph's Home at *Termonbacca*, Derry. It sits high on a hill and wherever you stand in Derry you look up and you can see its stark outline.

MY MOTHER COMING FOR ME

I vividly remember one day in particular of my eleven and a half years in *Termonbacca*. It was dinnertime and I had gone to get my dessert and the nun who was dishing this out stopped me and said, *"I have got good news for you"*. I was fourteen and a half at the time. The good news was that my mother was coming for me the next day and that I also had a brother. I was very happy at this news and I asked the nun where my mother was coming from and she curtly replied, *"Wales"*.

My heart sank as I immediately thought this was New South Wales in Australia. I knew that some of the boys from the home had been shipped out to Australia from *Termonbacca* in 1947. I thought this was going to be my fate because I was always being told that I was wild. The sister reassured me later that my mother was coming from a place in North Wales called Colwyn Bay. I was ecstatic to be getting out of this hellhole but at the same time I was frightened because I knew hardly anything of the outside world. I was also sad that I was leaving my friends who I considered to be my family. I cried myself to sleep that night in anticipation.

The next day came and I envisaged my mother to be six feet tall, beautiful and rich. What a shock I was in for. One of the boys called me, *"Brian, Brian. Quick your mammy's coming"*. I ran after him too scared to look myself. I said, *"What is she like?"* He replied, *"She's like a witch"*.

The nuns put her in the visiting room and came to fetch me. When the door was opened she was standing there with a bag in her hand. She was old, very dark haired and small. We were two strangers. She did not embrace me. She had merely come to collect me like a parcel. I was very hesitant to go with her but this was my escape from *Termonbacca*.

The nuns spoke to my mother and the next thing I knew I was walking down the hill away from *Termonbacca*. I was crying and crying as my friends waved me goodbye. I did not want to go with this strange woman. She was nothing like I imagined my newly found mother to look like. Then I heard her croaky voice say, "Now you wait 'till you meet your brother. His name is Tony". Anticipation set in. Please let him be nice. My mother took me walking up to the Creggan. I knew this area because the 'home boys', as we were known, always fought the Creggan boys. My mother had friends in the Creggan. She knocked on a door. An old lady answered it and we were ushered in. I saw a little old man sitting by a coal fire. Fear set in again. My mother sat down with these people and they talked for what seemed like hours. I was given a cup of tea. My mother took me to a very cold, dark room and told me to undress and get into the bed. Then she said that she would join me soon.

As I lay on the large double bed I could hear my mother talking downstairs. I could not make out what was being said and I must have dropped off. I awoke from my sleep later that night to find my mother lying in the bed next to me.

Once again I was frightened as to what I should do. I wanted to put my arms around her. This is what I thought I should do. I had never been this close to a woman before, especially one dressed in only her nightclothes. She was facing me and where the door was ajar a shaft of light was over her face. In this light I could see this old woman's face with black wiry hair. As I leant over her to take a closer look I could feel her hot breath coming from her open mouth. It smelt sweet and I though if I sucked this breath in I would get my mother's love. When I got up in the morning the feeling of love was not there. Only this cold woman. I was given a whole slice of toast to myself.

We left this friend's house and caught a train to Dublin where we got on a boat to Holyhead. I had never done anything as exciting as this before. I was a little bit scared but the thought that I was going to meet my brother was the main thing in my mind.

While we were on the boat I remember seeing a lot of men drunk and falling about. I went to the toilet and found a giant of a man being seasick. It was a cattle boat. When I came back from the toilet my mother was asleep. This gave me another chance to study her. As I was looking at her I knew that I did not love her and would never love her. I wanted so much for her to just cuddle me, tell me that she loved me and show me some affection and let me feel loved. But even then I knew this was not going to be. I felt as if I were merely a parcel she had just picked up and was going to deliver to my brother.

TO MY BROTHER IN WALES

Again I fell asleep. When I awoke my mother was peering at me. I asked her if my brother was like me. She said that I had his nose and then she started to talk to me about him. He was tall with blonde hair. When she said his name, *Tony* it was as if he were a saint. Oh how I longed to meet him, my brother. I was getting nearer. I was praying the train would go faster. I looked out of the train window. I could see the sea and sea gulls. After we reached a place in North Wakes called, Colwyn Bay we had to get a bus. Then we had to take a walk from the bus stop along a road that seemed to go on forever.

Finally we came to my mother's house. The house I should have lived in for fourteen and a half years, not in *Termonbacca*. My mother knocked at the door. An old man answered it. He was my stepfather. He said, *"Hello"* to me in a strange voice. My heart was pounding with excitement, fear and anticipation. Where was my brother? Would he like me? Would he cuddle me? Would he talk with a strange voice too? My stepfather, Bill told me that my brother had gone to the station to meet my mother and I but we must have missed him. I sat down for ten minutes waiting for my brother barely able to contain and control myself with excitement at the prospect of meeting him.

Suddenly the door burst open and my brother was there. Running to pick me up and cuddle me he put his arms round me. I was so happy. This was my brother, *Tony*. He said that he would look after me and I could feel his love and friendship just coming out from his heart. It was wonderful. Yes, he lived up to my dream of a brother.

After my mother put me to bed that night Tony came into my room to talk to me. He told me that he loved me and he would look after me and reassured me that I would never have to go back to *Termonbacca*.

The next day, my new found hero, took me all over the town telling everyone he met that I was his long lost brother. He was my brother. This was beyond my wildest dream. He was the greatest in the world, everything you could imagine a big brother to be.

He loved me.

THE COAL BUNKER

My memories of my childhood and early years are not the happy convivial ones that most adults can recall, but then I was not so fortunate as to have a family life. My childhood was spent in *Termonbacca* (a so-called home) for poor unfortunate children. Would you care to join me and follow me through some of my scary memories and some happy ones.

One of my most vivid memories is that of our chores in the Hell Home. At least three times a week, a group of about twelve young boys aged from 8 to 11 would have to polish the vast floors. We had to do this by all standing in a line and linking arms. Then, with polishing rags under our feet, we had to go up and down in a straight line polishing till we could see our reflections in the floors. The floors were red stone, and Cardinal Polish was put on them, and an older boy would recite the words, as we worked, *"River back, river back, Or, I will break the broom o'er your back"*.

We had two nuns standing watching us all of the time, making sure that we kept a straight line. If you did not, you would feel their wrath. You got a severe, sharp slap. I hated this work as did most of the boys, and to cause a stir and get out of the work, I upset the line of polishers.

My punishment was to be thrown into a pitch black dark hole, which I later learned was the coal bunker. I was terrified by the darkness and scared of what monsters this huge hole held inside it. All I could see in the darkness was the glinting eyes of rats staring at me as if I was their next meal. I screamed with fear each time I endured this hell hole which was at least 17 feet by 12 feet. Sometimes, one of the boys - *my pals* - would lift the door of the bunker just to let in the light momentarily for me. The nun would leave me there screaming for my life for half an hour. I had to promise to be good, just for the nun to let me out.

One time I was thrown in there and this time I did not scream as I had grown accustomed to this torture. Within minutes, to my amazement, I was being dragged out of the coal bunker and accused by a nun that the Devil was in me. My hair was naturally curly and this nun screamed at me, *"Look! The Devil's Horn!"* She then, took out a pair of scissors, and chopped and hacked all of my curls off. I complained to the Mother Superior about my treatment. She sharply replied to my face, *"You got what you deserved"*, and dismissed me.

GIRL PIDDLING ON FLOOR

I can clearly recall an incident which happened at one time at one of the schools I attended. This was Bishop Street School where we joined up with the girls. One day we were in a classroom and had formed a circle of girls and boys with a nun on the outside. We had to read and say the Catechism. One small girl interrupted the reading to ask if she could go to the toilet, to which the nun replied, *"No, wait till the Catechism is finished"*.

The poor wee thing rejoined the circle next to me, and from the corner of my eye, I could see her fidgeting, and, at the same time, a puddle began to grow larger on the floor.

Well, I just took her hand and ran with her. My intention was to get her to the toilet, but the nun stopped me in my tracks with a severe smack across the face that sent me flying. When I got to my feet I received a bashing from the cane. I can still see the sheer fright and fear in that girl's eyes.

ARM BREAK

I bet you all remember your school summer holidays with fondness and a smile. Well, here's an example of one of my summer holidays. All of us boys worked on a farm picking potatoes or some other manual task, e.g. feeding pigs etc.

One summer, in particular, we were all playing about first thing in the morning waiting to be driven to the potato fields on the tractor. I was larking around and fell off the tractor and hurt my arm badly. I was put to bed by a nun. As the day wore on my arm was swelling up more and more and growing more painful.

Eventually, it was decided to take me to hospital. Now, this was really exciting - a trip to the hospital. On arrival, I was seen by some nurses who were really kind and sympathetic towards me.

My arm was broken, and I was crying so loudly when the nurse told me, if I stopped crying, while they put my arm in a huge plaster cast, I would get a sweet. At the prospect of getting one sweet the tears stopped, and to my disbelief and shock, I received two sweets and a cuddle. I still remember the fresh smell of the nurse's uniform.

DIED

Whenever one of the Sisters died, she would be laid out in her coffin in the Chapel for three days before burial. We were forced to parade around her coffin which was open at least twice a day saying prayers. Another boy and I thought she was just asleep and imagined her getting out of the coffin when we left the Chapel to sit and have a cup of tea. Our imagination was running wild as was our curiosity.

One day, two of us sneaked into the Chapel to see if we could catch her moving or sipping tea. We were trying not to be frightened, pushing each other closer. We tickled her feet and to our sheer horror, she farted. She never moved, but a loud fart came out. We screamed and both ran faster than hares let out of a trap. Still shaking and out of breath, we ran and told all the other boys, *"She's only acting. She's not dead. We heard her fart"*.

FLYING

I remember when I was about ten years of age. It was a real windy day. It was a bad storm and we were ordered by the nuns not to go outside as the trees were being blown down. Myself and a friend decided not to heed the nun's warning and said we were going to fly away, if the wind was that strong.

We said our goodbyes to our pals, not wanting to come back as I knew that the next day I would be polishing floors and I would be put in the coal bunker again. Anyway, off we went. We scurried up the 28 steps to the street by the laundry holding each other's hands. We waited for the gust of wind to take us away.

Eventually, it came and, yes, up we went. We were flying. Our joy did not last very long. We were both lifted up about ten feet and thrown on to an embankment.

Our flying days were very short lived.

PROTESTANT CHURCH

When we were young, we were always warned by the nuns that we should never enter a Protestant church. We were not given any reason for this; just told not to go into the church.

On one occasion, I ran into a Protestant church, as my curiosity got the better of me. Yes, I was being nosy, and I wanted to see what their God looked like. It was a beautiful church, stained glass windows and lovely statues of Jesus. There were about seven or eight people in the church praying.

I noticed an old man mending one of the pews. As he was working, he was chatting to a lady. As I walked past them, they both said, *"Hello"* to me, instantly recognising me as a home boy because of the clothes I was wearing.

They asked me how long had I been in the home. I replied *"All of my life"*. I must have looked in a sorry state for the old man gave me a bag of sweets, and the lady gave me a sixpence and a cuddle.

I could smell the scent of daisy on the lady. It was very gentle and the smell of tobacco came from the old man. He told me to run along as I would get into trouble.

Well, with that sixpence in my pocket, I felt rich. I kept in my pocket for weeks just treasuring it. In my dreams I fantasised if either of them knew my mother or father. I did not spend the sixpence for three weeks. Eventually I did spend all of it in Maggie Doherty's shop near Bridge Street.

As soon as I spent it my happiness disappeared with it.

AFTER TERMONBACCA

I decided for myself when I finally left *Termonbacca* that I would get an education by attending night school. Then I knew I would eventually fit in with mainstream normality.

Yes, I wandered around for a few years in Wales, Manchester and various other cities digesting knowledge, and at the same time, looking for somewhere to settle down with, maybe, a wife and family. This happened in London where I have lived for the past 30 years, but my first marriage was not to be. My second marriage to my present wife is like a fairy tale come true. We married in a Registry Office on a freezing cold January morning 20 years ago, but the warmth of our love is intense. We have 11 grandchildren between us. When they ask a question, it is always in childlike innocence. So, when they ask of me, *"Grandad, what was Termonbacca like?."* how do I answer them: with a lie and tell them it was all sweet and honey, when deep inside of me, I know this was far from the truth. For the 11½ years I spent in *Termonbacca* I was reared up to feel as if I had committed a sin by being there. I was just another mouth to feed and to be chastised if I ever so much as thought for myself.

Not only should my grandchildren know the truth, but the good and generous people of Derry, who raised monies for us, should know, and be given an insight into *Termonbacca.* and the Nazareth House. I am not saying I do not have any fond memories of my childhood. I would be lying if I did. There were good times when we all went to *Buncranna* and were allowed to play like children, although, we were still under the watchful eye of one or two of the Sisters.

There were times when the American Navy men took us out and onto one of their ships. Another instance that brings a smile to my face is when one of the girls from the Shirt Factory hung out of the windows and gave us a wave, and a smile, and even threw us sweeties as we passed by in our uniform of home boys clothes. In these clothes we stood out very distinctly from other children in Derry.

My main inspiration for getting on with life has been my wife Barbara, who indulges most of my whims. I have always been interested in athletics and had a yearning to participate in sport at some level.

Well, the London Marathon was my opening. I kept on about how I would like to complete a marathon, so Barbara just threw down the challenge to me, *"Well, go on then. Run the marathon"*. This was just the start. I went on to complete 100 marathons. I hold the record for being the first man from Northern Ireland to complete 100 full marathons. I eventually joined a club made up of runners that met up at different races all over England, Ireland, Wales, Scotland and Sweden. We were simply called the 100 Marathon Club.

To gain entry to this elite club, each member had to prove with results that they had accomplished 100 full marathons. In fact, I took over from another running pal, the actual running of the club. This entailed writing, printing and sending out newsletters to all the club members. I purchased a silver trophy where all of our names were engraved as each new member achieved their glorious 100 marathons.

I made friends from all walks of life and I cherish those days.

List of Convents or the POOR SISTERS OF NAZARETH

ENGLAND. Bexhill: Birkenhead: Birmingham: Blackburn: Bristol: Brough: Cheltenham: Ditton: Finchley: Great Crosby: Hendon: Isleworth: Lancaster: Manchester: Middlesbrough: Newcastle-on-Tyne: Northampton: Nottingham: Oxford; Plymouth: Southampton: Southend-on-Sea: South-Sea: Wavertree (and St. Joseph's Home): Yelverton: Newbury.

IRELAND. Belfast and Nazareth Lodge: Derry and St. Joseph's, Termonbacca: Mallow: Sligo: Fahan: Portadown.
SCOTLAND. Aberdeen: Cardonald: Kilmarnock: Lasswade.
WALES. Cardiff: Criccieth: Swansea.
SOUTH AFRICA. Cape Town: Durban: Fourteen Streams: Johannesburg: Kimberley: Port Elizabeth: Pretoria.
RHODESIA. Salisbury.
AMERICA. Fresno: Los Angeles: San Diego: Van Nuys.
AUSTRALIA. Ballarat: Brisbane: Geraldton: Melbourne: St. Joseph's Home, Sebastopol: Tamworth: Launceston, Tasmania: Perth.
NEW ZEALAND. Christchurch St. Joseph's Home, Halswell.

In addition to the Novitiate at the Mother House. Hammersmith, London. W.6, other Novitiates have now been opened at Nazareth House, E Camberwell 6, Melbourne, Australia and also at Nazareth House, Los Angeles 64. California, U.S.A.

For the reception of aspirants to the religious life, Juniorates have been opened near Mallow, Co. Cork and Fahan, Co. Donegal, Ireland, and at Nazareth House, Hendon, London. N.W.4.

The following list is of the opening year of each Nazareth House, also the totals of children and elderly people who were cared for by each Nazareth House. Unfortunately, the list is not complete as many records are so old that they no longer exist, and I exhausted every avenue of research available to me.

Nazareth House	Opening Year	Total Children	Total Elderly
Hammersmith	1857	7709	5877
Aberdeen	1862	6040	1500
Cardiff	1872	6158	1450
Southend	1873	4598	1631
Oxford	1875	1500	1200
Nottingham	1876	1250	931
Crosby, Liverpool	1897	4154	972
Southsea	1883	2436	No Record
Bexhill	1890	2164	1518
Swansea	1905	800	No Record
Plymouth	1928	1300	No Record
Wrexham	1966	100	783
Birmingham	1910	2086	No Record

J.M.J.

Tel. 020 8748 3549
Fax 020 8741 4287

25th July 2003

Nazareth House
Hammersmith Road
London, W6 8DB

Dear Mr. Doherty,

I am pleased to send you the following information which you have requested, regarding numbers of children who migrated to Australia from Nazareth Houses in the North of Ireland. Nazareth House Belfast 50 children left for Australia:-

Girls 24	Sale dates
9	29 / 08 / 1947
8	8 / 05 / 1953
6	23 / 02 / 1955
1	24 / 12 / 1956

Boys 26	
1	29 / 08 / 1938
8	29 / 08 / 1947
3	18 / 03 / 1953
14	24 / 12 / 1956

Nazareth House Derry Sale Date

Girls 12		29 / 08 / 1947
Boys 50	2	17 / 02 / 1939
	27	29 / 08 / 1947
	21	28 / 01 / 1953

The Port of Embarkation was Tilbury, I do not have the names of the Ships. I hope this is the information you require for your book. You will understand that names or otherwise are confidential to each person.

With every good wish,

Yours sincerely,

Sister Hilary

Superior General.

Registered Charity No. 228906

Nazareth House		House Closed	Children Migrated to Australia
Hammersmith	1851		35
Aberdeen	1862		32
Cardiff	1872		26
Southend	1873		35
Oxford	1875		7
Northampton	1975		5
Nottingham	1876	2002	11
Middlesbrough	1880		8
Southsea	1883		nil
Cheltenham	1884		25
Bexhill	1890	2001	8
Kilmarnock	1891	2003	4
Isleworth	1892		14
Finchley	1897		nil
Crosby	1897		nil
Lancaster	1899		8
Swansea	1905	1997	72
Manchester	1905		nil
Wavertree	1909	2000	nil
Birmingham	1910	1990	37
Blackburn	1912		nil
Newcastle	1917	1998	14
Bristol	1921	1970	58
Carlisle	1925	1950	43
Bonnyrigg	1931		30
Southampton	1923	2001	108
Plymouth	1928		10
Bala	1937	1949	nil
Birkenhead	1945		nil
Criccieth	1949	1966	nil
Yelverton	1950	1965	nil
Wrexham	1966	2003	nil
Newbury	1954	1979	nil

BELFAST

On 9th May, 1876, the Bishop of the Diocese, Dr.Dorrian, brought the Sisters of Nazareth to Belfast, and rented to them his own residence in Ballynafeigh. The Bishop had been living in the house which now forms the front part of the Convent building.

It is interesting to read that one of the first old persons to come to Nazareth House was a Presbyterian lady, who applied for admission in 1876 in response to a Press advertisement which stated that the new House was open to the aged and the infirm irrespective of creed. She lived and died in her own faith and was regularly attended in the Convent by her Presbyterian minister.

The first sisters to come on the 9th May, 1887, with Mother St.Basil were: Mother St.Joseph *(McAuliffe)*, Sister Mary of Assisium *(Smith)* and Sister Mary of Bethlehem *(Carey)*. There were so many old people to be cared for that Mother St.Basil went back to Hammersmith and sent four more Sisters to help with the work. These were Sister Mary Hilarion *(Lennon)*, Sister Mary of the Incarnation *(Buckley)*, Sister Mary Pacificus *(Forbes)* and Sister Mary Matthias *(O'Connor)*. The work for the old people increased so rapidly that it as found necessary to build extensions; the last of these, St.Basil's, was blessed and opened by Dr. Philbin on the 9th November, 1966.

To keep abreast with the times and the changing pattern of child care, the Children's Wing was modernised and converted into self-contained flats for three groups of children. To date, the number of children cared for is 4,825 and old people 4,411.

DERRY

Mrs.Waters, a native of Derry, bequeathed £7,000 to the Bishop, Most Reverend John Keys O'Doherty, to found a home for the poor in the city. In 1891, he purchased a property, Sunnyside, consisting of a double house (one half of which was occupied at the time) and eight smaller houses in Bishop Street, for the sum of £3,360. He entrusted the management of the home to the Sisters of Nazareth. So, in February 1892, Reverend Mother General (Mother Mary of the Nativity), Mother M.Augustine, Mother Mary of the Visitation and five Sisters arrived to begin the foundation.

The pioneer Sisters were Sister Basil, Sister Berchmans, Sister Thomas, Sister Aquinas and Sister Kevin. They were warmly received by the Bishop, clergy and laity. The formal opening of the House by the Bishop took place on the anniversary of his consecration, March 2nd, 1892. In the early years of this century, a new wing for the children was built as there was no more room for them when their numbers greatly increased.

The top floor of the building was given over to the class children for dormitories, etc; the middle floor was occupied by the nursery children and the ground floor was used for classrooms.

Even in those days, there was a Government school in the House and the enrolment was over 200. Today, there is a Government-maintained School with over four hundred pupils (coming from all parts of the city) and sixteen fulltime teachers. An assembly hall was erected beside the School and was blessed and opened by Bishop Rev. N. Farren in 1956.

Meanwhile, the number of aged in the House had increased so much that the main building had to be extended. When the new Church was opened and blessed by the Bishop in 1962, renovations were carried out in the old Church, giving the old ladies more accommodation. Plans were drawn up for a new block for the men, as up to this time they were in very poor quarters.

Some few years had to elapse before this project could be carried out, as there were some occupied houses in the site and the tenants were not too keen on moving. However, the building was erected and opened in 1972. There is accommodation for forty and it is occupied by ladies and gents.

Many improvements have been carried out in the House over the past few years. A new kitchen has been built, the old ladies department has been very much updated and the children are now accommodated in three very beautiful flats.

Since the foundation of this House:-
The number of children cared for is   2.757
The number of old people cared for is   2,890

BELFAST LODGE

In April, 1899, negotiations began regarding the purchase of Fox Lodge on the Ravenhill Road, Belfast. It was up for sale, together with 10 acres of land surrounding it. The sale was completed in 1900 and Mother General, Mother Augustine, Mother Basil and Sister Constantia came to visit the newly acquired property, which later became known as *Nazareth Lodge*.

It was soon realised, however that the accommodation was quite inadequate for the two hundred boys now cared for under its roof, so it was decided to build a suitable house to accommodate them. This building was formally opened by Cardinal Lodge on October 15th, 1905.

In 1934, the Diocesan work for babies was taken over by the Sisters and the first baby, a girl ten days old, was received in the Lodge on October 16th In the same month, the old ladies and gents who had occupied the Lodge when the boys were moved into their new home, were transferred to Nazareth House and their apartments were converted into a nursery. When this building proved no longer habitable, it was demolished and a lovely new nursery, *"Bethlehem"*, was erected in its place.

The tiny babies, numbering at times up to 90, were, for a time, accommodated in the boys' recreation hall. However, a modern well-equipped nursery was built for them by the Diocese on ground adjoining the Lodge - the present St.Joseph's Babies' Home. It is still run by the Sisters.

The Lodge has now four family group units, catering for boys and girls. In the grounds there is a very flourishing nursery school and a beautiful well-equipped Primary School, St.Michael's, with an enrolment of 400. Since its opening, the Lodge has cared for 141 old ladies, 96 gents and 3,442 boys.

SLIGO

Nazareth House, Sligo, was opened on June 13th, 1910. His Lordship, the Most Rev. J. clancy, D.D., celebrated the first Mass there, at which Mother Clare of the Cross, Superior General, Mother Basil and the pioneer community were present. Mother Pudentiana, Sister Charles, Sister St.Brendan, Sister M.Edith and Sister M. ruperta formed the latter.

The Bishop was a kind friend and generous benefactor, and he showed a real fatherly interest in his new flock. The Ursuline Sisters were extremely kind, too, and each week they provided *Nazareth House* with a hamper of good things. The people of Sligo were glad to welcome the Sisters into their midst and since then have been most kind and helpful.

On June 30th, 1910, the first old lady, a Mrs. brennan, was admitted and since then 1,619 aged have made *Nazareth House* their home.

At the request of the Bishop, 17 boys were admitted from Sligo workhouse and so work with the children, which has been very successful in this House, was started. Until a few years ago, there was a very flourishing Infants' school on the premises.

Although *Sligo Nazareth* House was primarily a boys' home, it has now opened its doors to girls, and the are now 80 to 90 children. Good work has been done through the years with the boys and the Sisters who have looked after them must feel very proud of the number of Priests who can call *Nazareth House* their home. One boy, John Culien, will, D.V., be ordained in Sligo Cathedral by the Bishop, Dr.Conway, on June 18th, 1979.

Since 1910, 1,319 children have been in the care of the Sisters in Sligo.

TERMONBACCA

This house was founded on 2nd November, 1922. It was the estate of Sir Henry Millar. Finding that the building on the property was not large enough to accommodate 56 boys, the Sisters built an extension.

On the 1st November, 1922, Sister Elizabeth, Sister Kentigern and Sister Joseph Thecla and two boys left Bishop Street and took possession of the house. Mother Scholastica and Mother Brendan Mary came from Hammersmith. On 8th December, 1922, the first Mass was celebrated. Mother General and Mother Ireneus were present.

A few years ago, the old building occupied by the boys was levelled to the ground and rebuilt. To comply with the Social Services regulations in the field of child care, three group homes, each accommodating about twenty children, have now been set up. They are beautifully furnished and lack nothing to make them warm and comfortable - in fact, they are real 'family homes' for the boys and girls (yes, *Termonbacca* has opened its doors to these, too!) who live in them.

MALLOW

At the invitation of the Ministry of Health, Dublin, the Sisters, with the permission of His Lordship, Dr. Roche, Bishop of Cloyne, opened a Home for elderly people in *Mallow*, in September, 1930.

Newberry Manor was purchased on the 7th July, 1930, at a cost of £3,000, and on the 1st September, 1930, Reverend Mother General (Mother M. Macnise) accompanied by Mother Ireneus, Sisters Anthony Joseph, Stanislaus, Annunciation and Donatus left the Motherhouse en route for *Mallow* to begin the work of the new foundation.

The first Mass was offered in the House on 5th September and the Angelus was rung for the first time on that day. November 21st saw the arrival of the first old ladies. The number of aged seeking admission was so great that the house had to be extended and it now accommodates 200-300 old folk. The total number of elderly cared for since 1930 is 3,635

FAHAN

On 15th May, 1941, 46 babies were taken by bus from Derry to *Fahan*. Mother Elizabeth returned to Derry leaving two Sisters in charge of the house which had not been occupied for eight years. The next day some staff came from Derry, bringing with them five infants.

On Monday, 26th May, the first Holy Mass was celebrated in the house by His Lordship, Most Reverend Dr.Farren at 9am.
On the Feast of Christ the King, 1941, St.Mura's Postulancy was opened by Dr.Farren with Holy Mass at l0am, the babies having been meantime brought back to *Nazareth House*, Bishop Street.

Bishop Farren bought another house in the grounds which was used as a holiday house by the children from Bishop Street until it was decided, with the Bishop's approval, to use it as a Juniorate. This was opened on 25th May, 1954 and continued as such until 25th June, 1971. the building was then altered to accommodate old people and the first old lady was admitted on 4th July, 1974. At present there are 14 residents and there are plans for a new building to accommodate 40 aged.

Up to the present 1.238 babies have been admitted to the Nursery, and twenty three aged residents have been in the care of the Sisters

PORTADOWN

On February 12th, 1952, Very Reverend Canon McNelis requested Reverend Mother General to establish a home for needy children in *Portadown* in the Archdiocese of Armagh. A Miss Mary Josephine Marley had left a trust fund to the Archdiocese to be used for this purpose. The property purchased consisted of a house, now the Convent, and five acres of land.

On June 29th, 1953, two sisters - Sister Mary Coleman and Sister Eithna Mary were sent to *Portadown* and followed in September by Sister St. Ignatius. The community increased to five in January, 1954, when Sister Mary Ita and Sister Frances Bernard arrived for the collecting.

His Eminence Cardinal D'Alton visited the house on September 17th, 1953. He was delighted with the site and the surroundings and spent some time with the Sisters, bestowing words of encouragement and appreciation. Before leaving, he imparted his blessing, prayed God to bless the work too be undertaken and added, *"As it is God's own work he will surely bless it"*.

The first baby was received on 20th September, 1953, and three days later a few more were admitted. Due to a lack of space, thirteen was the number decided upon as a limit. Needless to say the cots were very quickly occupied. The new building is beautiful, airy and spacious, but as we all know babies are scarce these days. 998 babies have been admitted since the foundation.

REGIONAL HOUSE, DUBLIN

This foundation came from the Hand of God. Though the desire to start a foundation in Dublin was uppermost in the minds of Mother General and the General Councillors for many years, other more needy causes elsewhere claimed the personnel and finance available. However, in this time of decentralisation, it was considered necessary for the betterment of the Congregation to establish regions in the Home countries as well as abroad, so the need for a central House in Dublin was keenly felt.

God provided an opportunity. Miss Kathleen Gahan, 27, Leinster Road, Rathmines, feeling the weight of her years, called her solicitor to draw up a will. As she did not wish her house to be lessened in appearance in any way, she decided to leave it to a Community of Sisters doing charitable work in Eire. She asked her solicitor to draw up a list of Communities, and our Congregation happened to be sixth on the list of ten. She picked ours, she knew not why, as she had never met our Sisters, not had she any connection with us. A letter asking if we would accept the house was sent by the solicitor to Mother General and, though at the time it looked a long term affair, she agreed to do so.

Miss Gahan died unexpectedly on 4th November, 1965, and the Sisters moved into the house in 1966. Mother General and her Councillors decided to make it a *Regional House*, where a few Sisters could study in preparation for the various works of the Congregation.

DUBLIN

At the time of Miss Gahan's death, Archbishop McQuaid was in Rome, so a letter was forwarded, through a priest friend of the Congregation, to Rome, acquainting him of the situation. A quick reply was received, in which an appointment was made between the Archbishop and the priest in January, 1966. His Grace received Mother General and her companion very kindly. He seemed very pleased and made full enquiries as to what work they intended to do. On hearing that they wished to open a Home for the Aged, as the most urgent need, His Grace gave, not only his blessing to the proposal, but he also gave Mother General the choice of a very fine site which was left to him as a Trust (part of the O'Brien Estate with frontage along Malahide Road) - flat ground that needed little preparation.

On October 7th, 1967, the site for the new house was blessed by Monsignor Fitzpatrick, V.G., and was blessed and opened by His Grace, Archbishop McQuaid on 7th May, 1970. Present at the opening were:- Reverend Mother St. Donatus, Mother General, Mother Mary Gobnait, Mother Regional, Mother Alphonsus Joseph, Vicaress, Mother Fidelis of the Cross, Bursar General and Mother M. St. Gertrude, Superior.

The Irish Region was officially inaugurated and the first Meeting held at the Regional House on 7th October, 1969, Feast of the Holy Rosary of Our Lady. To mark this historic occasion and bring down the blessing of God on the Region, a special Holy Mass was offered by Reverend Alphonsus Mahon, C.Ss.R., Provincial Procurator.

Present at the mass were: - Mother Alphonsus Joseph Kelly (representing Mother General (Mother St. Donatus Hanbury), Mother Mary Gobnait O'Leary, Regional Superior, Mother Teresa Catherine Maginn, 1st Regional Councillor, Mother Francis Benedict Keane, 2nd Regional Councillor and the community at Leinster Road.

DERRY JOURNAL ARTICLES

The following pages are news reports taken from the Derry Journal newspapers from the years 1892 to 1931. I hope this will give people a better insight into *Termonbacca* and the *Nazareth House*, Derry.

A lot of the news reports have been shortened as they were so large. I did not have the room in my book to accommodate them. If you are interested and want to read any that I have not put down, just go into your local library and ask for backdated copies of the *Derry Journal*.

To make it easier for you, the reports are dated yearly, weekly, daily and page numbered. This will save you all the extensive time-consuming effort it took me. The photographs shown were also in the *Derry Journal* and I have been granted copyright permission by the newspaper to reproduce theses photographs.

They start in 1927 till 1982 and are of the children who passed through *Termonbacca* and the *Nazareth House*, Derry. I feel I should apologise to you if you are part of a photo, but were not in either of these institutions. It was very hard for me to tell who was in the home or who was not. Please accept my apologies.

There are some images copied for you from an old book by Miss J.Giblen written in 1927. these are of *Nazareth Houses*. I have searched every avenue possible, but cannot find a living relative of this lady.

THE DERRY JOURNAL, MONDAY MORNING.

FEBRUARY 29, 1892.

THE POOR SISTERS OF NAZARETH IN DERRY.

FORMING A HOME.

Thanks to the charity of the late Mrs. Waters, a Home is now being prepared in Derry, where under the care of the Poor Sisters of Nazareth many of the aged and infirm poor will find rest and comfort for the remainder of their days. On Wednesday next (which by a happy coincidence chances to be the anniversary of his consecration), the Most Rev. Dr. O'Doherty will formally open the Home. During the week a few old persons will be admitted to its shelter. The entire premises not yet being available for occupation, some months must necessarily elapse before the institution gets into complete working order.

Nazareth House, Hammersmith, London, of which the new foundation at Sunnyside is a branch, was founded by Cardinal Wiseman in 1857. During the 41 years of its existence it has made astonishing progress in the development of its various branches of charity. There are now 18 houses of the Order, where no less than 5,000 poor—men, women, and children—find home, food, clothing, and, perhaps, best of all, the kind, motherly care of the Sisters. Though they have only one house in Ireland—that at Ballynafeigh, Belfast—the Sisters are, nevertheless, no strangers to Ireland, for they are one and all in the Order Irishwomen, and one need hardly add that in the houses which they have erected in Great Britain and the Colonies, many a poor old exile from Erin and many a poor Irish orphan has found home and happiness.

THEIR WORK.

Who will be admitted into the Home? The rules answer: (1) The aged and infirm destitute poor, and (2) orphan, deserted, or incurably infirm children. The term "aged poor" means men over 70 and women over 60. The term "infirm poor" includes all those, no matter what their age, who are prevented by bodily infirmity, or the results of accident, from earning their bread. Hospital work cannot, however, according to the rules of the Order, be undertaken; neither can a temporary home be offered, unless in exceptional cases to young Catholic girls—when sick, homeless, friendless, or out of employment. Such duties appertain more to the Mercy than to the Nazareth Nuns. It is, however, to be hoped from God's mercy that the day is not far distant when some good charitable person whom He has blessed with means will do for the young, homeless, and unemployed, as well as for the sick, the delicate, and the injured, what Mrs. Waters has so nobly done for the "aged and infirm." That the dawn of the 20th century, now so near at hand, may behold in full working order in Derry Columbcille a Mercy Hospital and a Mercy House is surely not too wild a dream. "But," interrupts the critic, "suppose you had these various establishments built, equipped, and in full working order, how are you to keep them going?" We answer, "The streamlets of Catholic charity which annually trickle out of Derry are more than amply sufficient if united, turned into and confined within the proper channels, to ceaselessly turn the wheel of all these various institutions, whose establishment the full organization of Catholic charity in Derry demands."

To the aged and infirm destitute poor Nazareth House offers a permanent home. The old people are not, however, to be rigorously confined within the convent walls. Every month, during certain hours, their relatives may visit them at the Home, and once each fortnight they are free to call upon their old friends and neighbours through the city. In case of sickness, of course, friends have free access at all times.

THE CHILDREN'S HOME.

Besides providing as far as space permits for the aged and infirm, Nazareth House offers a home, with all a mother's care, to the little ones— boys or girls who have been deprived of or deserted by their parents. Boys cannot, however, remain longer than seven or eight years old, unless a special wing be added to the home. Girls may remain until fourteen years of age. Should they (the girls) in after life, by reason of sickness or need of employment, want a temporary home, they are always made welcome to return for a while. Children suffering from incurable maladies are also received and cared for, if need be, all their lives. But as is obvious, medical reasons forbid the admission of imbeciles or persons suffering from fits. The Sisters hope, as time goes on, to establish a *creche*, where the babies of working women will be cared during work hours. This feature, so prominent in the manufacturing towns of Germany, where female labour is largely employed, should prove a welcome boon to many a young working woman in Derry. "The Sisters do not confine their labours within the walls of their convent. Their ministering extends far and wide. The maimed and diseased come daily to the convent to have their wounds and sores dressed, and to procure remedies for their various ailments." Furthermore, in Derry they purpose when invited by priest or doctor to visit the home of the patient, and as far as possible discharge for them their various offices of charity. 'Tis for such patients the Sisters ask, and are glad to receive donations of linen rags, bedclothes, clothing, &c. The Sisters of Nazareth have neither lay sisters nor servants of any kind in their houses. They themselves fulfil, with pleasure and affection, every office, even the most menial which charity can suggest, or human infirmity may require towards their poor charges, caring for each of them with the tenderness of a mother, making their beds, washing their linen, cleaning their rooms, cooking their food, and becoming *literally beggars in their stead*—all for the love of Him who embraced poverty in order to teach mankind to serve Him in the persons of His poor.

THE DERRY JOURNAL, MONDAY

MARCH 7, 1892.

THE NAZARETH HOUSE IN DERRY.

The *Weekly Register*, referring to the establishing of the Nazareth House in this city, says:—"On Wednesday evening the Rev. Mother General, accompanied by the Rev. Mother Augustine, left Nazareth House with the Sisters to open the new Home for the poor in the historic city of Londonderry, at the request of its zealous Bishop, the Most Rev. John Keys O'Doherty The Sisters who will form the community are Sisters St. Basil (Superior), Sisters Constantia, St. Maurus, Berchmans, Th. of Aquin, and Kevin; and they will be encouraged to labour in their own dear land by the blessing of the venerable Vicar-Capitular, and by the remembrance that their new house was sanctioned by their great friend and father, the late Cardinal (Manning) not long before his death. Though they will not have the consolation of hearing precious parting words from his own lips, as so many of their Sisters have done, nevertheless they may hope that his blessing will follow them, as in the days when he was moved to tears at the sight of these Irish ladies, in their youth and beauty, breaking all ties of flesh and blood to labour in the service of Almighty God." We *(Derry Journal)* have to inform the charitably disposed that as some aged persons will be received into the Home to-day, the Nuns will be glad to receive donations of clothing suitable to the needs of old people.

THE DERRY JOURNAL,

DECEMBER 28, 1898.

CHRISTMAS AT THE NAZARETH HOUSE, DERRY.

Amid the joys and pleasures usually associated with the Christmas festival, it is pleasing to be able to record many kind acts of generosity and benevolence on the part of the public towards those less fortunately circumstanced. The various public institutions in which the wants of the sick and the poor are cared for never fail to obtain all the requirements for the spending of a joyous Christmas by their inmates, and perhaps to no other establishment of its kind in the city is the support and sympathy of friends extended in such a whole hearted manner as to the Nazareth Home. As in former years the many friends and well-wishers of the Home—including all creeds and classes—this year sent valuable and useful donations for the usual Christmas festivities. On Christmas day the number of visitors to the Home was considerably greater than that of former years, the great centre of attraction being the beautiful Crib, which as usual occupied a position in the Sanctuary of the Home Chapel. Needless to say the Nativity Scene as here depicted called forth the warmest admiration from the constant stream of visitors who thronged the building during the day. The beauty and splendour of the design as well as the realistic character of the entire picture, make it an object at once reverential and impressive. The good Sisters of the Home showed every attention to the visitors, conducting them to the beautiful little chapel, where the Crib has been erected, as well as through the several apartments of the House. On Monday evening a concert was given in the Home by a number of local artistes, whose efforts to interest and amuse the old people and children were highly successful and warmly appreciated. Last evening the inmates were again entertained by a number of friends.

The Sister Superior and the other Nuns at the Nazareth House feel deeply grateful to all the kind friends who so generously assisted them with presents of various kinds, which were utilised with marked success in enabling both the children and the old and infirm inmates to appreciate the Christmas festivities.

FAHAN

The House at Fahan had become known as the Orphanage; a place where babies of as young as a few days are brought to await suitable adoption. That was the purpose it served after the former stately Brewster home overlooking Lough Swilly was acquired by Bishop Farren for the Sisters of Nazareth. Over several years, it did splendid work. The devoted Community threw itself wholeheartedly into this great humanitarian crusade for which there had been a crying need. Its record is a proud one. Children committed to its nursery are, indeed, lucky; a short time and they are entrusted to the fosterage of families who give them a proper upbringing.

My visit to Nazareth House in Fahan within days of Christmas impressed me as proving how completely the good nuns and their domestic staff can create that atmospheric quality of "homeliness" which makes the residents count their blessings and thank God for their good fortune in being there.

The House is now much more than a refuge for orphans, it also looks after as many of the aged as it can accommodate. The Superior, Mother Michael, told me of the limited space in which they have to work and what a blessing it would be if additional room were provided. Now that the Health Board has "recognised" their work and is sending geriatric cases to them from time to time, she is hopeful that, before long, something will happen to enable them to extend the scope of their work for the elderly.

At present, there are fourteen men and women being looked after (all over eighty). One lady, in her ninety-fifth year, I found in excellent health and spirits. So much so that when an impromptu entertainment was staged on my visit, she was one of the residents who needed no coaxing to have her telling a succession of quaint stories that had everybody in fits of laughter!

In both departments, Mother Michael told us, there are waiting lists. Nazareth House in Fahan is the kind of exceptional place that the elderly long to find a "corner" in. But with facilities as they are, no more can be accepted. The Community hopes that, in time, it will be possible to find the funds to provide extra accommodation. The need is pressing, because, despite the best efforts of St. Joseph's, which caters for over 200 requiring institutional care, there are many others in dire need of the superb services that Fahan House provides.

I can speak from personal knowledge of the excellence of the food and services which the residents enjoy. No Grade A hotel could outpoint the culinary skills of the kitchen staff, the luxurious accommodation, the comfort, the informality and the assiduity of the nuns and their helpers in really brightening the lives of those in their charge.

Derry and Donegal need no reminding of the good work of the Sisters of Nazareth and the input of well spent funds needs to be greater still in these inflationary days, especially in a place where nothing is done by halves and where stinting, for stinting sake, is anathema.

Take, for example, the Nazareth House at Fahan. I was there before, and you will have read something of the impressions I brought away. It's a unique place of rest, comfort, sympathy and loving care for people who cannot fend for themselves. It's not an institution with an impersonal air about it, where rigidly applied rules and regulations reduce the inmates to mere acquiescing cyphers in an unvarying routine which excludes real happiness from within its walls. (Which is not to imply that all institutions are organised and run on such a soulless basis. In Donegal, that dreaded word "institutionalism" has, in later years, little or no application.)

NAZARETH LODGE VISIT BY MAYOR MAKES HISTORY

HISTORY was made in Belfast's Nazareth Lodge yesterday when, for the first time in the 101 years of its existence, it was visited by the Lord Mayor of Belfast.

Councillor James Stewart and his wife Dorothy accepted an invitation from SDLP Councillor Mr. Liam Hunter to visit the Ravenhill Road orphanage where he was reared along with five brothers and a sister.

When she arrived, the Lady Mayoress was presented with a bouquet of flowers from one of the children and following his presentation, the Lord Mayor and his wife were brought on a tour of the building by the nuns who run it.

During the visit, the Lord Mayor said that he was delighted he had taken advantage of the opportunity to visit the orphanage and was "most impressed and surprised" by what he saw.

'So happy'

"I am really surprised that the whole place is so homely and the children are all so happy. There is none of the usual institution atmosphere about it all," he said.

The orphanage is run by the Sisters of Nazareth for boys and girls who are in need of care or who have been deprived of their parents. A nursery and primary school are attached to it.

The original building was named Fox Lodge and was built in 1857 by a Belfast solicitor Mr. James Young, who lived there with his family for 20 years.

It was given the name Nazareth Lodge in 1925 when the nuns from Nazareth House — a home for orphan and destitute children — took it over. In 1957 the old building was demolished and new premises were built on the old site.

The newly appointed Mother Superior of the home—Reverend Mother Thomas Aquinas —said she found it hard to believe that this was the first visit of a Lord Mayor to the Lodge.

She has just recently returned from England, where she has been for a number of years, and she said that it was common practice there for the Lord Mayors of each town to visit children's homes, especially at Christmas.

JUNE 29, 1931 — PAGE

SISTERS OF NAZARETH.
ST. JOSEPH'S HOME, TERMONBACCA.

NEW ORATORY BLESSED BY BISHOP.

Yesterday his Lordship, Most Rev. Dr. O'Kane, blessed the new Oratory attached to St. Joseph's Home, Termonbacca. The ceremony of the blessing was followed by High Mass, the celebrant being Rev. Joseph O'Doherty, B.A., S.T.L., St. Columb's College; deacon, Rev. D. L. M'Laughlin, B.A., B.D., do.; sub-deacon, Rev. Francis Collins, D.Ph., do.; and master of ceremonies, Rev. Eugene O'Doherty, D.D. His Lordship the Bishop occupied the throne in the sanctuary, and among the clergy in the choir were Very Rev. Dr. Farren, President, St. Columb's College; Rev. M. Smyth, P.P., Iskaheen; Rev. Wm. Murphy, St. Brendan's Seminary, Killarney; and Rev. T. E. Maguire, C.C., St. Eugene's Cathedral; Rev. Patrick O'Brien, C.C., Long Tower; Rev. Bernard Smith, C.C., Waterside; Rev. James O'Flagherty, Ecclesiastical Inspector; Rev. J. M'Glynn, C.C., Waterside. The music of the Mass was rendered by the Boys' Choir, under the direction of Rev J. B. M'Cauley, B.A., Chaplain to the Convent. The music of the Mass was entirely Gregorian, and not merely reflected great credit on the choirmaster, but demonstrates the possibilities of Gregorian Chant even in the case of juvenile choirs. After the Mass Solemn Benediction of the Blessed Sacrament was given by his Lordship the Bishop, who also blessed the Statue of St. Joseph—a beautiful piece of sculpture —erected in the grounds of the Convent.

The new chapel has been made possible by the generosity of Mr. J. J. Madden in erecting a new and commodious dormitory for the boys. Mr. Madden has been the constant friend of the Sisters since the foundation of the Convent in Termonbacca. He assisted them in all their activities. He had already supplied the hostel for the senior boys, and more recently still, has installed a central heating system for practically the entire Convent. Mr. Madden's attentions are not confined to the material structure. Year after year he has been instrumental in providing an outing for young and old, both of St. Joseph's Home, Termonbacca, and of Nazareth House, Bishop Street. The new dormitory is equipped on most modern lines, and is ideally situated overlooking the Foyle. This extension has made it possible for the Sisters to utilise the older building for the purpose of a chapel to replace the original one, which had become totally inadequate for the numbers.

After lunch the Bishop and priests were entertained to a very enjoyable concert by the boys. Several items were supplied by the Boys' Brass Band, under the direction of Mr. J. Durnin, the energetic and capable conductor.

FAHAN ORPHANAGE

The main Nazareth House building at Fahan built in 1871 for the Colhoun family and later it came into the ownership of the Brewsters, who used it as a residence for a number of years. (We could not help admiring those stained glass windows which the latter had put in—and bearing their initials—at the top of the stairway.)

This spacious dwelling had been vacant for a number of years and its introduction to the Sisters of Nazareth came in 1939 when forty babies were evacuated from Nazareth House in Derry and accommodated there during the war years. All this happened through the good offices of Bishop Farren and when it was seen that this manor house was ideally adapted for the special purposes of an orphanage, both in accommodation and location—overlooking Lough Swilly and amid the loveliest surroundings—his Lordship acquired the former Brewster home and handed it over to the Sisters of Nazareth to establish a foundation in Donegal. The children evacuated from Derry in those war-torn years enjoyed Fahan immensely as a holiday home.

The house was retained by the Order and some years later His Lordship conferred another special favour when he acquired a second house in the same grounds and handed it over also to the Sisters. For some time this was utilised as a

THE DERRY JOURNAL, MONDAY MORNING, OCTOBER 27, 1941

SISTERS OF NAZARETH
Opening of First Irish Novitiate
Most Rev. Dr. Farren Celebrates Mass at New Home in Fahan

THE Lord Bishop of Derry, Most Rev. Dr. Farren, yesterday celebrated Mass in St. Mura's, Fahan, in connection with the acquisition by the Sisters of Nazareth of a new Home and the opening thereat of the first Novitiate House of the Order in Ireland.

The occasion marks the beginning of a new and notable chapter that will be written by the zealous members of this Order in the historical annals of Fahan. These annals have as their central figure St. Mura, after whom, very appropriately, the nuns' new house is named.

Adjacent is the site of the ancient Abbey which St. Mura founded in the seventh century—a monastery which for many centuries afterwards flourished as a centre of piety and learning. St. Mura came from the other end of Ulster to found here by the shores of Lough Swilly his famous monastic school.

Now the Nazareth Nuns have come to historic Fathan Mura and opened a house for the reception of postulants wishing to devote their lives to God's service through His poor and orphan children. Their undertaking gives every promise of being blessed with success, writes our representative.

Lough Swilly stretched placidly out towards the Fanad hills and October sunshine bathed the secluded grounds where I stood on the steps of the ornate mansion whose outlines looked the statelier for its position against the wooded background and beyond that heather and moss-covered slopes. Such was the scene that had claimed my admiration when the tinkling of a bell diverted attention from the scenic beauty of my surroundings.

In one of the mansion's spacious apartments the renovation and equipment of which as a chapel had just been completed Mass was about to begin.

The celebrant was Most Rev. Dr. Farren, Lord Bishop of Derry, who was thus solemnly putting his seal on a project quietly undertaken and as quietly carried on to fruition by his Lordship himself, to give to the Sisters of Nazareth a new home and to Ireland the first Novitiate House of the Order.

Assisting the Bishop at the Mass were Rev. Dr. E. O'Doherty, Vice-President, St. Columb's College, Derry, and Rev. D. M'Laughlin, Dean, dc.

Other priests present were Very Rev. Joseph O'Doherty, President, St. Columb's College; Rev. J. M'Caughey, Chaplain, Nazareth House, Derry, and Rev. Con Doherty, Chaplain, Nazareth House, Fahan.

It is some months now since St. Mura's, Fahan, came into the possession of the Order. The Superiors immediately concluded that no better use could be made of it than a house for the reception of Irish postulants who, owing to war-time travel restrictions, find it increasingly difficult to reach the head house at Hammersmith. How splendidly fitted for the purpose is St. Mura's was seen by a "Journal" representative yesterday when he was privileged to be present at the simple but deeply impressive ceremonial which marked the visit of his Lordship to beseech through the Mass God's blessing on the notable enterprise.

One could not imagine any more beautiful environment or a house and situation more befitting the worthy object they are now to serve.

Their acquisition will mark a new chapter in the annals of the Order, whose work in the interests of God's poor not only in Ireland but in many far-flung Mission fields is too well known to need any commendation here.

The Mother General, being unable to travel, was represented at the formal taking over some time ago by the Mistress of Novices from Hammersmith,

under whose direction the preparations for the reception of postulants have been carried out. Despite the difficulties of the times, the whole interior has been transformed and the ardour and enthusiasm with which the Sisters have set about their task—for a task it has been in existing circumstances—is reflected in the fact that already a few postulants have presented themselves and everything is in readiness to receive a number who have been on a waiting list for some time.

The work had the utmost encouragement from the Lord Bishop whose deep practical interest in the well-being of the Order, as well as his appreciation of the great and self-sacrificing zeal which characterises the Sisters, is manifested in this proud development of the Order's activities in Ireland.

According to an inscription on a wall in one part of the extensive grounds, it would appear that the estate was laid out in 1871—exactly seventy years ago. The grounds, in which there are many large out-houses, wooded tracts and gardens, extend for about a mile back from the main road and slope gradually up to the mountain lands in the background.

The following priests visited St. Mura's yesterday afternoon—Very Rev. P. Tracy, P.P., V.F., Buncrana; Rev. J. M'Bride, P.P., Fahan; Rev. P. O'Brien, C.C., Buncrana; Rev. W. Dolan, C.C., do.; Rev. H. M'Faul, C.C., do.; Rev. H. M'Keague, C.C., Fahan; Rev. B. Kelly, C.C., Burt.

St. Mura's Nursery, situated in the grounds of Nazareth House at Faham, which will now accommodate the children

1892

Monday, February 29th 1892; *(page 5)*.
Poor Sisters of Nazareth in Derry forming a home.

Monday, March 7th 1892; *(page 5)*.
Nazareth House.

Wednesday, December 28th 1892; *(page 8)*.
Nazareth House, Bishop Street.
On Monday evening, the children, supported by nuns in the Nazareth House in Bishop Street, were afforded an evening's Christmas entertainment A large number of toys were brought together by the children of the well-to-do in the city, and these were presented to the little inmates of the Nazareth House, who were afforded an hour of enjoyment. Rev Father McMenamen administrator of St Columb's Parish represented the clergy.

1895

Wednesday, February 13th 1895; *(page 5)*.
Nazareth House, Deny was given a most handsome donation from the Most Reverend Dr. O'Doherty. He said *"I have great pleasure in sending you a cheque for £25"*.

Friday, March 15th 1895; *(page 2)*.
The Poor Sisters of Nazareth. The aged poor that in men over 70 and women over 60 with no means of support, deserted orphans or incurable infirm children. 150 inmates provided for. Donations please.

Monday April 1st 1895; *(page 5)*.
The Nazareth House. Nazareth Nuns in Cardiff in Wales received £127 19s 5½d

Wednesday, August 7th 1895; *(page 5)*.
Nazareth House Derry visited by Mrs F. Auldel Phillips, wife of the Governor of the Irish Society.

Friday, August 30th 1895; *(page 5)*.
Nazareth House Derry. Proposed concert meeting of the Representative
Gentlemen was held in the Library of St Columb's Hall.

Monday, October 7th 1895; *(page 5)*.
The Nazareth House Deny. In our advertising columns today the Sisters of Nazareth make graceful acknowledgement of the services of all who aided in promoting and supporting the recent concert held in St Columb's Hall on behalf of their institution. The amount real issued is £36 5s, a very creditable sum, to be applied to the most deserving charity dispensed by the Sisters.

Monday, December 9th 1895; *(page 8).*
Nazareth House Derry, enter the Convent Chapel. Descended to the schoolroom were sixty little boys and girls.

1896

Wednesday, January 1st 1896; *(page 8).*
Nazareth House Derry. Grateful thanks for the £4 10s 9d given for the benefit of the Home by the Celtic Combination Company.

Wednesday, January 8th 1896; *(page 8).*
Nazareth House tea party given by Dr Byrne J.P. and Mrs Byrne.

Friday, July 3rd 1896, *(page 5).*
Nazareth House Derry. On Tuesday, the children cared for by the Nazareth House were treated to a trip down the lough on board the steamer Jeannie Deans. This was arranged at the invitation of a local Catholic gentlemen who does not wish his name to be mentioned, whilst the manager of the steamship company. Mr Gibson the officer on board from the popular Captain Doherty and over 100 children were on this trip.

Monday, August 3rd 1896, *(page 5).*
Nazareth House and the Irish Society.

Friday, August 7th 1896; *(page 5).*
Nazareth House and the Irish Society.

1897

Friday, January 5th 1897; *(page 5).*
Nazareth House Derry for St Anthonyes Bread.

Thursday, May 17th 1897, *(page ?).*
The Nazareth House and orphan children.

Friday, December 1897; *(page 5).*
The Christmas Crib, Nazareth House. Three carpenters made this the previous year and brought it back this year.

Friday, December 31 St; 1897; *(page ?).*
The Christmas festival entertainments at the Nazareth House Derry. Very long article on the Sisters praising them.

1899

Monday, January 2nd 1899; *(page 5).*
The Nazareth House annual entertainment on Saturday evening was one of the most enjoyable entertainments of its class which has been held in Derry for many years.

This was held in the large assembly room of Nazareth House Derry. The programme may shortly be described as that of a ballad instrumental concert. The organisation of this was in the hands of the most popular comic Mr J. P. Coyle.

Wednesday, June 19th 1899; *(page 5)*.
Nazareth House Derry. The annual excursion of the children under the charge of the Sisters of Nazareth Derry was held yesterday to Molville. The little excursionists were under the guidance of the Mother Superior. The children marched in order to the quay by way of Bishop Street, then Shipquay Street and then Foyle Street. Mr Henry Thompson was partaken of the rain and came when the entire party retired to Temperance Hall.

Monday, September 18th 1899, *(page 5)*.
The Nazareth House. There was a very creditable act by the workmen of Derry. Recently, owing to the pressure on the accommodation of Nazareth House, as also in regard of the desirability of having something of an open space in a situation rapidly being built on, there was acquired a valuable property of two fields. These, however, were only enclosed by an intergarden hedging, which was inadequate to present purposes, and a paling forming a proper enclosure became necessary. The extent of these fields made this an expensive undertaking and so presented a difficulty to the Sisters, who, however, were not without friends capable and willing to do a generous part. Twelve Derry artisans, hearing of the matter, at once tendered their service and when the sisters accepted the volunteers, they set to work and had the fields thoroughly enclosed with wood palings, giving their labour for eight days totally free of all cost. The paling measures 521 feet and is 10 feet high all around. The work is very well done and this work will be better appreciated when we mention the fact that it was all done when the men had done their ordinary day's labour. It was all done after these hours. They heartily gave to this undertaking the time they had for recreation and rest and everyone will accord them honour for it.

Monday, October 9th 1899, *(page 5)*.
Nazareth Home Derry. An appeal to all those who love God's poor. The inmates at present number 270. Subscriptions may be sent to the Derry Journal's office in Shipquay Street or to the Sister Superior, Nazareth Home. Big write up for a new wing. Bishop most reverend D. O'Doherty a municified donor of £100.

Wednesday, October 11th 1899; *(page 5)*.
Nazareth House. An appeal to all who love God's poor in order to enable to pay off a very heavy debt. Repeat.

Friday, October 13th 1899; *(page 5)*.
Nazareth House. The friends and relations of the Sisters of Nazareth House at home and abroad will be glad to hear that they have received from the Holy See the third and final confirmation of their work and constitutions and the Bishops in England, Ireland, Scotland, Wales, South Africa and Australia in whose Diocese the Sisters have Houses.

Friday, October 13th 1899; *(page 5)*.

The Nazareth House. *Further subscriptions.*

Monday1 October 16th 1899; *(page 5).*
The Nazareth House Fund. Further generous subscriptions.

Wednesday, October 18th 1899; *(page 5).*
The Nazareth House. Further subscriptions to this fund.

Friday, October 20th 1899; *(page 5).*
The Nazareth House Fund.

Monday, October 23rd 1899; *(page 5).*
The Nazareth House Fund. Collected £424.

Monday, October 23rd 1899; *(page 5).*
The Nazareth House Deny. An appeal to all who love God's poor. Very large write-up.

Wednesday, November 1st 1899; *(page 5).*
The Nazareth House Fund. The amount already acknowledged is £499.

Friday, November 3rd 1899; *(page 5).*
Two separate articles and write-ups. The Nazareth House Fund reached £599. Both write-ups were on the same page.

Monday, November 6th 1899; *(page 5).*
The Nazareth House Fund reached £599.

Monday, November 6th 1899; *(page 5).*
The Nazareth House Deny. Grand Annual Concert. Large write-up.

Wednesday, November 8th 1899; *(page 5).*
Nazareth House. Grand Annual Concert held in St Columb's Hall.

Friday, November 10th 1899; *(page 5).*
Nazareth House. Brilliant concert in St Columb's Hall. The occasion was the fifth annual concert in aid of the truly noble and beneficial work done by the Nazareth House. Miss Louie Rental-Boal, who for quite a number of years has been a leading favourite at the Nazareth House Concerts, sang "Scenes that are Brightest" and "Killarney". Beside these 170 little children there were 90 elderly people. Very large write-up.

Monday, November 13th 1899; *(page 5).*
Nazareth House Friday night concert. Very big write-up.

Friday, November 17th 1899; *(page 5).*
Nazareth House Fund. Total at November 16th : £702 15s 0d.

Friday, November 24th 1899; *(page 5).*
Nazareth House Fund. Total: £714 13s 0d.

Wednesday1 November 29th 1899; *(page 5)*.
Nazareth House Fund.

Friday1 December 1st 1899; *(page 5)*.
Nazareth House Fund:- £834 3s 0d.

Friday, December 22nd 1899; *(page 5)*.
Nazareth House Fund. Splendid result of the concerts. The Nazareth House was handed a cheque for £102 and a successful concert in St Columb's Hall brought in another £30.

Monday, December 25th 1899; *(page 5)*.
Nazareth House. The Catholic Benefit Society, St Columb's, Branch number 37, has kindly forwarded to us through its secretary Mr James Logue £1.

1900

Wednesday, January 3rd 1900; *(page 3)*.
Midnight Mass was held in the Nazareth House Derry.

Friday, January 12th 1900; *(page 5)*.
The Nazareth House Fund stands at £1,019 5s 0d.

Monday, January 22nd 1900; *(page 5)*.
The Nazareth House Fund received further donations. The total now is £1,023 5s 0d.

Friday, January 18th 1901; *(page 5)*.
The Nazareth House, Omeau Road, Ballynafeigh, Belfast. The following letter has been forwarded for publication. Chichester Park, 6th January 1901, Fox Lodge as a Home for Orphan Boys, 160 old and infirm men and women and 320 orphan children.

Wednesday, April 24lh 1901; *(page 5)*.
Nazareth House. A charity football match in aid of funds?. On Saturday a grand exhibition football match will take place at Celtic Park. when Hibemians and Celtic will meet for the purpose of aiding the commendable charity of the Nazareth House. The kick off will be at 3:30. The grandstand is to be solely reserved for ladies. A very interesting feature in connection with the match, apart from the good object in view, is that the St Patrick Splendid Waterside Band will be present and perform both prior to the match and during the interval after the first half of the play. The wonderful and superb playing of this band at the local feis on Saturday last has been the subject of praise in every part of the city and to hear these clever musicians again will be surely a treat in itself. It is hoped a big attendance will turn out at the occasion.

Monday,April 29th 1901; *(page 5)*.
Celtic versus Hibemians in aid of the Nazareth House. St Patrick Drum and Pipe Band Waterside. Celtic (2) goals; Hibemians (nil).

Wednesday, July 10th 1901; *(page 5)*.
Nazareth House.
From the children's excursion the following are the subscriptions received at this office until this date 10th July. The Long Tower £1, the High Sheriff of the City, Maxwell Solicitor, the children of St Columb's Girls School and the employees of Derry Journal £1.

Friday1 July 12th 1901; *(page 5)*.
The Nazareth House excursion.
A lot more names. Total raised £36 17s 6d.

Wednesday July 17th 1901; *(page 5)*.
Nazareth House - Tribute to St Anthony.
Their cordial gratitude expressed to all benefactors who contributed to the fund for the Orphan Children's Annual Excursion.

Wednesday August 21st 1901; *(page 5)*.
Nazareth House.
Excursion at Ballyliffin selected on the Cardonagh Extension Line. A large write up.

Friday August 23rd 1901; *(page 5)*.
Nazareth House. They erected the tent which had been kindly given by the
Foyle Rope Work Company, Messrs Watts and Co., Derry.

1902

Monday February 24th 1902; *(page 5)*.
A gift to the Nazareth House.
Letter sent to the Editor of the Derry Journal with kindness from the young men of the Ivy Athletic Club. A gift of £7 10s 0d for the Nazareth House.

Friday May 30th 1902; *(page 5)*.
Nazareth House Derry.
A new wing to be added to the Nazareth House. Mr D. M. Caifrey, the well-known builder from Strabane, who is in charge of the work. The new wing is being of freestone, with moulded string courses, sills, pilasters, and the dimensions are 160 feet long by 100 feet wide, and four storeys high. The building trade have been provided for by the architect Mr E. J. toye. The work, when complete, will cost about £1,600.

Wednesday July 30th 1902; *(page 5)*.
Nazareth House.
Children's excursion by an outing to which the little ones were treated. The now favourite seaside resort of Ballyliffin was chosen for the excursion and the party of little boys and girls numbering upwards of 200 left on the Swilly Railway for the station.

Monday September 8th 1902; *(page 5)*.
Nazareth House Derry.
His Eminence Cardinal Moran was at the Nazareth House. Big write up.

Monday October 13th 1902; *(page 5)*.
Nazareth House.
The Annual Concert will be held in St Columb's Hall on Thursday and Friday December 11th and 12th. Ticket prices will be 2s 6d and 1 shilling.

Friday December 5th 1902; *(page 8)*.
Nazareth House. Annual concerts at St Columb's Hall on the 11th and 12th. Big write up on the forthcoming event

Wednesday December 10th 1902; *(page 5)*.
Nazareth House.
Thursday and Friday night concerts will be held in St Columb's assembly hall.

Friday December 12th 1902; *(page 8)*.
Nazareth House, Derry.
Eighth annual concert. Big write up.

Monday December 15th 1902; *(page 7)*.
Nazareth House concert.
The second concert in aid of Nazareth House took place on Friday evening.

Wednesday December 24th 1902; *(page 8)*.
Nazareth House.
Crib at Nazareth House Derry.

1903

Wednesday January 7th 1903; *(page 7)*.
Nazareth House. A meeting of ladies was held on Monday in the library of St Columb's Hall to promote the entertainment in aid of the building fund for the Nazareth house.

Friday January 16th 1903; *(page 5)*.
Nazareth House Derry.
Conversation to be held at St Columb's Hall in aid of the building fund of the new wing for the Nazareth House. An excellent musical program has been arranged.

Monday February 2nd 1903; *(page 5)*.
Nazareth House.
Tomorrow evening conversazione St Columb's, a group of elderly people. There are inmates of 76 women 25 men and 190 children, making a total of 291 in care at the institution.

Wednesday February 4th 1903; *(page 5)*.
Last night's conversazione brilliant scene in St Columb's Hall. Large write up.

Monday February 16th 1903; *(page 5)*.
Nazareth House Derry.
In the Opera House Derry, the Derry Drama Club played in aid of the Nazareth House.

Friday September 11th 1903; *(page 5)*.
Nazareth House Derry - the annual concerts.
There were 207 children and 119 elderly people attending.

Monday November 9th 1903; *(page 5)*.
The Nazareth house held their ninth annual concerts.

Monday November 16th 1903; *(page 5)*.
Concert series was an initial success, repeated. Large write up.

1905

Monday May 1st 1905; *(page 5)*.
Nazareth House fete - making preparations - successful meeting. The home which shelters over 200 children and nearly 100 aged poor persons. The ladies of Derry and district have kindly rounded themselves together to raise, by means of a fete on the 27th, 28th, 29th and 30th June, for the next new wing they need, donations of at least £1,200.

Wednesday 3rd May 1905; *(page 5)*.
Nazareth House fete.
A bric-a-brac kiosk at the home1 a very novel and interesting event, is advertised to take place in St Columb's Assembly Hall on Thursday evening 11th The proceeds will be in aid of the furnishing fund of the new wing of the Nazareth House for which the forthcoming fete is being organised.

Wednesday May 10th 1905; *(page 5)*.
Nazareth House fete.
Attractive entertainments are to take place in St Columb's Assembly Hall tomorrow, Thursday, evening at 7:30. Tickets are priced at 2s 6d.

Wednesday May 10th 1905; *(page 5)*.
Football. The Nazareth Home.
A benefit match between Derry Celtic and the Pick of Derry will take place at Brandywell Road on Saturday, 13th, May. The match starts at 3:30.

Friday May 12th 1905; *(page 5)*.
Nazareth House Fete.
The Fete in St Columb's Hall last night was a great success.

Monday May 15th 1905; *(page ?)*.
The Nazareth House Benefit Match.
The object of the game was to help the Nazareth House building fund. The game ended with Celtic 3 goals and Derry nil.

Monday May 22nd 1905; *(page ?)*.
Nazareth House Fete.
A Geisha Kiosk and Musical Reunion in St Columb's hall on Tuesday evening the 30th.

Friday 26th May 1905; *(page 5)*.
Nazareth House Fete.
The Musical Reunion next Tuesday evening, 30th, in St Columb's Hall. Stalls tickets are still on sale.

Monday 29th May 1905; *(page 5)*.
Nazareth House Fete.
For tomorrow night at St Columb's Hall - the entertainment.

Wednesday 31st May 1905; *(page 5)*.
It is announced that a Drama Entertainment, under the auspices of the Irish Stall, will be given in St Columb's Minor Hall, on Tuesday 13th June, for the Nazareth House Fete. The admission is only 15d.

Wednesday 31st May 1905; *(page 5)*.
The Nazareth House Geisha Kiosk.
One of the most popular items was an Irish Dance by a Miss J Cothoun and Master A Brestin.

Friday 2nd June 1905; *(page 5)*.
The Nazareth House Fete is attracting an outing of many.

Monday 12th June 1905; *(page 5)*.
Nazareth House Fete.
By special permission "Amorelle" was produced on Friday evening last, in aid of the Nazareth House Fete. Special trains were run on the evening as there was a crowded attendance at the Opera House.

Monday 12th June 1905; *(page 5)*.
Nazareth House Fete.
There was a meeting of lady members, who were working in connection with several kiosks.

Monday 19th June 1905; *(page 5)*.
Nazareth House Fete.
Ladies appeal for children's day, also the new wing extension for Nazareth House. As already advertised, the new wing for the children of Nazareth House will be formally opened by Dr O'Doherty, Bishop of the diocese, on Tuesday 27th June. Subscriptions in aid of the building fund will meanwhile be gratefully received and acknowledged by the Sisters at the Nazareth House.

Friday 23rd June 1905; *(page 5)*.
Nazareth House.
A Fete was held in the new garden.

Monday 26th June 1905; *(page 5)*.
The Nazareth House Fete will be opened tomorrow in aid of the Furnishing Fund of Nazareth House. The Fete opens at 3 o'clock. A very big column on this.

Friday June 30th 1905; *(page 7)*.
Continued success; brilliant results. Very big write up.

Monday July 3rd 1905; *(page 5)*.
Nazareth House Deny.
Tribute to the good Sisters. Thousands were present on Friday and Saturday. Very big column.

Wednesday July 5th 1905; *(page 5)*.
Nazareth House.
General meeting of the ladies of several kiosks held in the Nazareth House on Sunday evening 9th July at 4:30.

Friday July 14th 1905; *(page 5)*.
Nazareth House.
The ladies of the Irish Stall in another column return thanks, to Mr H. Coil and the members of the Deny Dramatic Club also to Mr J. Linch and Mr Cunningham for valuable assistance given the Stall in connection with the recent Fete.

Monday July 17th 1905; *(page 5)*.
Nazareth House.
A pleasant evening in the Nazareth House. Derry Drama Club on Wednesday evening gave a performance to the inmates of the Nazareth House.

Monday October 9th 1905; *(page 5)*.
Nazareth House Deny.
Entertainment will take place on the 14th - 15th December next in St Columb's.

Monday December 4th 1905; *(page 5)*.
Annual Concert for a great city charity on Thursday and Friday 14th and 15th. 300 orphans, all children, to attend.

1906

Monday April 6th 1906; *(page 5)*.
Nazareth House.
Help at Easter.

Monday November 12th 1906; *(page 5)*.
Nazareth House.
Letter to the editor.

Monday November 12th 1906; *(page 8)*.
Nazareth House Winter Fete.
The Masque will be run on December 11th and 13th at 2 shillings and 1 shilling.

Wednesday November 14th 1906; *(page 5)*.
Nazareth House.
A series of entertainments conversazione on the 20th December at St Columb's Hall. The ladies of Derry are noted for their zeal and eagerness.

Friday November 16th 1906; *(page 5)*.
Nazareth House. Children's Masque in St Columb's Hall. Tickets can be obtained from Mr Frank Coghtan, photographer, of 31 Carlisle Rd or Mr James McCann, Beechwood Street.

Wednesday December 7th 1906; *(page 5)*.
Nazareth House Grand Winter Fete - full particulars. It is anticipated to be a brilliant pageant.

Monday December 12th 1908; *(page 5)*.
Nazareth House Winter Fete: the coming Conversazione on Monday evening. A meeting of the ladies engaged in the work of the coming conversazione.

Monday December 17th 1906; *(page 8)*.
Winter Fete - a letter to the editor of the Derry Journal.

Wednesday December 19th 1906; *(page ?)*.
Nazareth House Winter Fete Conversazione - tomorrow evening. An anticipated brilliant and attractive function in St Columb's Assembly Hall.

1910

Friday March 25th 1910; *(page 5)*.
Nazareth House Derry.
Attention is directed to our advertising column, announcing two performances of "Sweet Lavender" in St Columb's Hall on Tuesday and Wednesday, that is the 5th and 6th of April, of the Nazareth House Derry. The play is a very pretty one and is seldom attempted on the amateur stage. On this occasion however a very talented combination has been secured and as rehearsals have been in progress for sometime it is anticipated that an excellent and enjoyable performance will be the result.

Friday April 7th 1910; *(page 5)*.
Nazareth House - "Sweet Lavender" in St Columb's Hall. Rehearsals for the Hall's forthcoming performance of (`Sweet Lavender" in St Columb's on Tuesday and Wednesday.

1912

Friday February 9th 1912; *(page 8)*.
Nazareth House Derry - proposed Summer Carnival.
At a meeting held in the Nazareth House on Sunday last, it was decided to hold a Summer Carnival towards the end of June in aid of the funds of this very deserving institution. No doubt the idea of having an outdoor display in the Summer will commend itself to all. Various suggestions were made as to how the entertainment could be rendered most attractive, but eventually, consideration of the matter was adjourned for a fortnight, when it will be further discussed and the final arrangements made. The adjourned meeting will be held on Sunday 18th at 4:30 in the Nazareth House. The promoters look forward to a big attendance of ladies and gentlemen in this good work on the occasion.

Friday February 16th 1912; *(page 5)*.
Nazareth House proposed outdoor Entertainment. Cards of invitation have been sent out.

Monday February 19th 1912; *(page 5)*.
Nazareth House - Grand Entertainment launch meeting.

Friday April 19th 1912; *(page 5)*.
Nazareth House Fete. As already announced a Grand Dance under the auspices of refreshments stall will be held in St Columb's Hall on Monday night.

Monday April 22nd 1912; *(page 5)*.
Nazareth House. Picture Palace Entertainment is announced in today's Grand Benefit Exhibition for the Nazareth House Fete. This will be given in the new Picture Palace in Shipquay Street.

Friday April 26th 1912; *(page 5)*.
Nazareth House Fete Picture Palace entertainment. The management of the Picture Palace Shipquay Street very kindly gave a benefit performance last night in aid of the 'Bric a Brac' stall in connection with the Nazareth House Fete. Mr Bronson is the manager.

Monday April 29th 1912; *(page 4)*.
Nazareth House Fete, Monday night. A most successful dance was held in St Columb's Hall, which was organised by the ladies who are in charge of the Bonbon and the Smokers' stalls.

Friday May 17th 1912; *(page 5)*.
Nazareth House Fete. Music and merriment will be the leading features in the Outdoor Entertainment being given in the Nazareth House grounds.

Friday May 22nd 1912; *(page 5)*.
Nazareth House Fete. Fete jumble sale and dance to take place tonight. Doors open at 5:45, admission is 3d.

Monday May 27th 1912; *(page 5)*.
Nazareth House Fete. Jumble sale and dance a success. The dance was held in St Columb's Hall.

Friday May 31st 1912; *(page 5)*.
Nazareth House Fete. Another picnic to the Ness.

Wednesday June 12th 1912; *(page 5)*.
Nazareth House Fete. An interesting hurling contest will take place tomorrow. Sarsfield Band will discourse a selection of music and there will be a Bonbon and Smokers' stall.

Friday June 14th 1912; *(page 5)*.
Nazareth House Fete. A Grand Fete is to be held in Nazareth House Derry on the 27nd, 28th and 29th June 1912. This promises to be a brilliant success.

Monday June 17th 1912; *(page 5)*.
Nazareth House Fete. An immense success is assured.

Wednesday June 19th 1912; *(page 5)*.
Nazareth House Fete. Full programme outlined.

Friday June 21st 1912; *(page 5)*.
Next week's Fete in aid of the Nazareth House. A galaxy of attractions is being arranged for the Grand Fete.

Monday June 24th 1912; *(page 5)*.
Nazareth House claims on North West. Support for Grand Fete gives opportunity to manifest appreciation.

Wednesday June 26th 1912; *(page 5)*.
Nazareth House Grand Fete - opening tomorrow.

Friday June 28th 1912; *(page 5)*.
Nazareth House Derry. Grand Fete opened, showing the unselfish work of the sisters. Also a noteworthy tribute by The Most Reverend Dr I. T. Hugh and the Mayor of Derry Mr M. Farland.

Friday July 19th 1912; *(page 4)*.
Nazareth House Fete. The winding up meeting in connection with the Nazareth House Fete. The stallholders' returns were £900 although their expenses were well over £100.

Friday August 2nd 1912; (page 4).
Sir Alfred and Lady Newton paid a visit to the Nazareth House, also the Mayoress, Mrs M. Farland.

Monday December 23rd 1912; *(page 2)*.
Nazareth House. The Sisters of Nazareth mourn the late Clement K. Scott, the famous journalist, of the London Daily Telegraph.

1913

Friday April 25th 1913; *(page 4)*.
Nazareth House Derry. Cinematograph display in St Columb1s Hall. The London Motion Company is giving two night performances in aid of the Nazareth House.

Monday April 28th 1913; *(page ?)*.
Tonight in St Columb's Hall there is a benefit for the Nazareth House by the London Motion Company.

Monday October 20th 1913; *(page 5)*.
Nazareth House Deny is holding its Annual Dance and tickets will be on sale priced 5 shillings: singles at 3 shillings.

Monday November 10th 1913; *(page 4)*.
Nazareth House Deny. Their Annual Dance will be held in St Columb's Hall on November 19th.

Wednesday December 31st 1913; *(page 5)*.
Nazareth House - the Benefit Football Match has been postponed.

1916

Monday January 31st 1916; *(page 4)*.
We are glad to learn that the all of the first issue of tickets for the fixtures have been disposed of and that a second issue is being prepared. This speaks well for the success of the Entertainment, which is being organised in a manner that can result only in a most enjoyable and brilliant evening. Apart, however, from the merit of the hall, the cause of charity calls for a generous response on the part of the citizens who know the excellent work that the Sisters of Nazareth carry on for the aged poor and the orphan children and we are sure that the call will not be in vain and that the returns for tickets on this occasion will be in excess of those of previous years.

Monday February 28th 1916; *(page 3)*.
Nazareth House, Derry. Grand drawing of prizes will take place in the Lecture Room of St Columb's Hall.

Friday March 3rd 1916; *(page 5)*.
Nazareth House, Derry. Grand Drawing of prizes. There are twelve prizes in all. The tickets are only sixpence. You can buy them in several of the city shops.

Monday March 16th 1916; *(page 8)*.
Nazareth House, Derry. Grand Draw of Prizes (a reminder to all readers)

1917

Monday October 1st 1917; *(page 3)*.
In aid of the Nazareth House - the members of the Aileach Dramatic.

Monday November 26th 1917; *(page 5)*.
Nazareth House. Christmas Crib at Nazareth House.

1919

Wednesday January 1st 1919; *(page 4)*.
Nazareth House, Derry. Annual Ball at St Columb's Assembly Hall.

Monday January 6th 1919; *(page 2)*.
Nazareth House. Annual Ball on Wednesday night.

Wednesday January 8th 1919; *(page 3)*.
The Nazareth House Annual Ball is tonight.

Monday January 27th 1919; *(page 3)*.

Nazareth House. St Columb's Hall Annual Ball.

1920

Thursday December 31st 1920; *(page 5)*.
Nazareth House Ball was a splendid success. Over 800 people attended.

1921

Monday January 17th 1921; page 3.
In aid of the Nazareth House - a successful entertainment. The Annual Entertainment organised under the auspices of St Columb's Total Abstinence Society was held on Friday evening last, 14th January. St Columb's Hall being in the possession of the military, it was decided to hold the evening in the Foresters' Hall, Henrietta Street. The entertainment which took place was in the form of a whist drive and was most successful. The proceeds collected were donated to the funds in aid of the Nazareth House.

Monday December 19th 1921; page 5.
Nazareth House Derry - Annual Ball in aid of the Friends.

Friday December 23rd 1921; *(page 5)*.
Nazareth House, Derry - Sister Jubilee of crib open to the public until 12th January.

Wednesday December 28th 1921; *(page 2)*.
Nazareth House Ball promises to be an exceptionally attractive fixture.

1924

Monday January 7th 1924; *(page 4)*.
Nazareth House Ball is to be held in the Guildhall.

Monday September 29th 1924; *(page 1)*.
There is a whist drive tonight in the Guildhall in aid of the Nazareth House.

Wednesday October 29th 1924; *(page 5)*.
Nazareth House Fete held in the Guildhall.

Monday November 24th 1p24; *(page 8)*.
Nazareth House Christmas tree.

Friday November 28th 1924; *(page 5)*.
Nazareth House Fete Ball.

Wednesday December 10th 1924; *(page 4)*.
Nazareth House Christmas tree.

Friday December 12th 1924; *(page 8)*.
City Cafe.

1925

Monday January 7th 1925; *(page 5)*.
Nazareth House Ball - the forthcoming social event will be held in the Guildhall.

Thursday January 16th 1925; *(page 2)*.
Nazareth House Ball was a brilliant function in the Guildhall. 1000 people were in the hall.

Saturday January 19th 1925; *(page 7)*.
Cakes and bread are baked in the Nuns' bakery. Thirty years age there were 150 inmates. Today the family has grown to 400 in the Nazareth House.

Friday March 13th 1925; *(page 9)*.
Nazareth House Fete. A stall.

Wednesday May 27th 1925; *(page 5)*.
Nazareth House Fete - tomorrow evening cruise.

Monday June 22nd 1925; *(page 5)*.
Nazareth House Fete.

Monday July 6th 1925; *(page 5)*.
Nazareth House Fete.

Wednesday July 29th 1925; *(page 8)*.
Nazareth House Fete. Final meeting.

1926

Monday January 11th 1926; *(page 3)*.
The Nazareth House held a successful Whist Drive in the Guildhall.

Wednesday January 13th 1926; *(page 5)*.
Nazareth House held a Whist Drive.

Monday February 8th 1926; *(page 4)*.
A Grand Operetta is planned in aid of the Nazareth House.

Friday February 12th 1926; *(page 5)*.
Nazareth House, Derry. St Columb's Hall was crowded last night when the Operetta (Pepin the Pippin) was staged by students of St Columb's in aid of the funds for Nazareth House.

Monday March 1St 1926; *(page 2)*.
A whist drive in aid of St Joseph's, Termonbacca was held in the Rossville F.C. Rooms on Friday night. This was a splendid success and on the whole a very pleasant evening was given by the Rossville Football Club.

1931

Monday January 5th 1931; *(page 5)*.
Nazareth House Ball the forthcoming function at the Guildhall. In connection with the refreshments it has been decided to hold a cake competition. Six valuable prizes have been presented to the committee.

Wednesday January 14th 1931; *(page 5)*.
The Nazareth House Ball. This was a successful revival of the large Guildhall Company. 600 people were present. The last Annual Ball in aid of the Nazareth House was held about 6 years ago. Supper was served.

Friday November 27th 1931; *(page 11)*.
Nazareth House Collection. The Nazareth House Nuns, Deny are this week making their annual collection in aid of their Home for Orphans and Aged People. During their stay in the parish, they are guests of the Very Reverend Cannon Gallagher P.P.O.F. This is one of the annual collections that the people subscribe to most ungrudgingly, recognising the greatness and holiness of the work of the good Sisters.

Monday December 28th 131; *(page 5)*.
At the Nazareth House, and also at Termonbacca, the observance of the festival of Christmas was in every way appropriate to the boys and girls and the aged inmates who were provided with a special Christmas treat and spent a very enjoyable time on Friday and the following days. There were many visitors to both Houses and in both Houses the beautiful cribs were objects of much interest, as they had been artistically constructed. Their devotional nature was most effective.

1932

Wednesday December 21st 1932; *(page 5)*.
May the Devine Child of Nazareth reward our kind friends and benefactors and give them every Christmas joy and many blessings in 1933. Sincere and heartfelt thanks to all from the Sisters of Nazareth, Derry.

I can hear what you are saying to yourselves,

"My, this looks easy. All he's done is photocopy everything from a newspaper".

Well, let me put you all straight on this matter. If only it had been that easy. Myself and my wife have scoured our way through 12,000 old copies of the Derry Journal in the British Newspaper Library.

Some of the papers were in such bad condition through age that they could not be handled, so we had to look at them on microfilm. Each week we have had to travel a very lengthy journey to the Newspaper Library, taking with us a packed lunch as sometimes we would be researching for the duration of 6 hours.

We were both endlessly sifting through huge ledgers of newspaper just trying to find one little snippet of news or a photograph regarding Termonbacca or the Nazareth House to relay to you.

You all have different perceptions of how the two homes were run and how we were treated by the Sisters. I can only give you my account of how it was in Termonbacca. Although there were many different aspects to our upbringing. I can only speak about how I was treated. I cannot speak for others and what happened to them.

I know in my heart that I would not put a child of mine in one of these institutions and make them endure such cruelty that I feel I suffered.

THE NAZARETH HOME BOYS' BAND, WHO PLAYED ON BOARD THE STEAMER.

1928

CHILDREN FROM THE NAZARETH HOME IN THE FUNERAL PROCESSION

THE DERRY JOURNAL, FRIDAY MORNING, JULY 5, 1920 - PAGE 4

1929

THE DERRY JOURNAL, MONDAY MORNING, APRIL 20, 1931

THE POLYPHONIC ORCHESTRA, DERRY,

Which in conjunction with other Derry artistes, gave a concert last evening in the Nazareth House, Bishop Street. The photograph, taken outside the institution, includes the conductor, Mr. Joseph O'Doherty, and one of the soloists, Miss Attie M'Ginley. The other soloists were Miss Maura M'Closkey, Mr. Joseph O'Doherty, the conductor, also played (ventriloquism and character sketches), and Miss Margaret Back (dances), Mr. Jack Collins (songs), Mr. Joseph Hunter violin solo. The accompanist was Mrs. E. H. O'Doherty. The splendid programme was greatly enjoyed. The Polyphonic Orchestra secured very high marks (and the cup) at this year's Feis Doire Colmcille.

1931

ST. JOSEPH'S BOYS' BAND FUND,
Termonbacca, Derry.

APPEAL FOR NEW INSTRUMENTS.

Please Give !   **Every Little Helps**

DERRY JOURNAL, FRIDAY MORNING, AUGUST 2 1947

Emigrating To Australia

These boys, ages ranging from five to twelve years, will shortly leave St. Joseph's Home at Termonbacca, Derry, for Australia, under an emigration scheme which has the approval of the Catholic Hierarchy. In the land of their adoption most of the boys will be placed under the care of the Irish Christian Brothers, and the younger ones will continue under the care of the Nazareth Sisters.

DERRY JOURNAL, WEDNESDAY MORNING, JULY 2, 1947

NAZARETH HOUSE CHILDREN'S OUTING

Children of the Nazareth House, Derry, who had their annual outing on Monday, photographed in the grounds of the Nazareth House, Fahan.

The Derry Journal, Friday, April 14, 1950

A group of young Irish dancers from the Nazareth House, Derry, who competed at Feis Doire Colmcille.

APRIL 1952

Little girls from the Nazareth House, Derry, who formed choirs which competed at Feis Doire Colmcille. One of the choirs won the Teachers' Perpetual Challenge Cup for girls' choirs. Also in photograph is their conductor, Mr. Jas. McCafferty.

APRIL 1953

Outstanding Feis successes were scored recently by these children from the Nazareth House Convent P.S., photographed with Mr. James McCafferty, musical director, and Mr. Brendan De Glin, dancing instructor. Their successes at Feis Doire Colmcille were: 1st and 2nd, girls' unison choir; 1st, junior action song; 1st, Gregorian choir; 2nd, girls' three-part choir; 1st, 2nd, 3rd, girls' trio; 1st, country dance (under 15); 2nd, country dance (under 11); 3rd, double jig (under 8). Their successes at Feis Ailig, Bunerana, were: 1st and 2nd, girls' unison choir; 2nd and 3rd, girls' trio; 3rd, girls' solo (8-12 years). In the Feis Doire Colmcille Gaelic section they had 1st, 2nd, 3rd, Bun Rang; 3rd, story-telling; 2 ties 3rd place junior history; 1st, senior history. At Feis Ailig they provided the 1st, two 2nds, 3rd, Irish language.

HOLIDAY TIME, TERMONBACCA, DERRY. 1953

The annual Christmas party for children at the Nazareth House, Bishop Street, was held yesterday. Most Rev. Dr. Farren, Bishop of Derry, attended and distributed gifts to the tiny tots. Also in the picture are Sister Aidan and Rev. F. O'Doherty, Chaplain.

1953

TREAT FOR DERRY CHILDREN - 1954

THE DERRY JOURNAL, MONDAY, 15th MARCH, 1954

Girls from the Nazareth House, Derry, who were entertained on board the U.S.N. destroyers, Meredith and Johnston, at Derry on Saturday.

On Saturday afternoon eighty boys and girls from Nazareth House, Derry, were taken on a visit to two United States Navy destroyers, the Meredith and Johnston, which are at present making a short stay at Derry.

A section of the children went to each ship and were shown over the vessel by members of the personnel, including Protestant Chaplain Alfred Saeger, who had charge of the arrangements. They were given a film show during their two and a half hours on board and were also entertained to ice-cream and cake. The film show included cartoons for children.

The visit terminated at four o'clock, when thanks were expressed to the Americans for their hospitality to the children by Rev. F. O'Doherty, Chaplain, Nazareth House.

The party comprised fifty girls from Nazareth House and thirty boys from St. Joseph's Home, Termonbacca. The boys, on board one destroyer, were shown films that included "The Story of Robin Hood," and the girls, who were on the other destroyer, were shown "Son of Paleface" and other films.

Those who made the local arrangements for the visit included Mr. William Crowe.

[Our photograph above shows some of the children with members of the crew. Standing on the right is the Rev. Saeger and on the left Rev. F. O'Doherty, Chaplain, Nazareth House, and Mr. Robert Ennis, who was in charge of the boys.]

Children of the Nazareth House Convent P.S. Derry, who, following up their success at Feis Doire Colmcille, at which they won the Bishop's Shield, awarded annually to the school securing the highest aggregate of points, also scored an impressive list of successes at the recent Feis Ailigh in Buncrana. Their successes at Feis Doire Colmcille were 1st Junior Action Song; 2nd Senior Action Song; 2nd and 3rd Girls' Unison Choir; 2nd 3-Part Choir; 1st Country Dance (under 18); 2nd Country Dance (under 15); 1st, 2nd, 3rd Bun Rang (Section 1); 1st, 2nd, 3rd Bun Rang (Section 2); 2nd Gaelic Verse-speaking; 1st, 2nd, 3rd Junior History and Father John O'Doherty Memorial Cup; 1st, 2nd, 3rd Senior History. Their Feis Ailigh successes were—1st Action Song; 1st and 3rd Girls' Unison Choirs; 3rd Girls' Solo (12-15 years); 1st, 2nd, 3rd Bun Rang; 2nd Story-telling (12-14); 3rd Gaelic Verse-speaking (12-14); 2nd Irish History; 2nd English Verse-speaking (12-14); 2nd and 4th Embroidery; 2nd and 3rd Crafts.

THE DERRY JOURNAL, FRIDAY, 2nd JULY, 1954

Boys from St. Joseph's, Termonbacca, provided music and plenty of colour with their tableau, "Ten Little Nigger Boys," in the Long Tower Carnival parade through the streets of Derry.

1955

Termonbacca Boys' Home Concert

Most Rev. Dr. Farren, Bishop of Derry, was guest of honour at the first concert staged in St. Joseph's Boys' Home, at Termonbacca on Friday. Seated among the children who, with their attention rivetted on the stage, present a charming study in expressions, his Lordship has on his left Rev. Mother Bridget, Superior, Termonbacca, and on his right Rev. Mother William, Superior, Bishop St., and Rev. Mother Anthony, Superior, Fahan.

THEY WERE SUCCESSFUL AT FEIS AILIGH

Holy Family Choir No. 2, Nazareth House, Derry, winners of the girls' choir competition at Feis Ailigh with 92 marks.

CHILDREN'S CHRISTMAS PARTY
WEDNESDAY MORNING 28th DECEMBER 1955

These children from the Nazareth House were among a large number of youngsters entertained at the annual A.B.C. minors' Christmas party and free film show held in the Rialto Cinema, Derry.

Children from the Nazareth House were to the fore in this section of the throngs which lined Bishop Street to greet the Cardinal as he proceeded to St. Columb's College for yesterday's reception there.

THE DERRY JOURNAL, FRIDAY, 30th DECEMBER, 1955

Most Rev. Dr. Farren, Bishop of Derry, photographed yesterday with children of the Nazareth House, Bishop Street, to whom he distributed gifts at the conclusion of their annual Christmas-time entertainment. Also in picture are Rev. Mother M. William (left) and Sister M. Aidan.

PRIZEWINNING CHOIR

The Nazareth House, Derry choir which took first place in the girls' choir competition at Feis Doire Colmcille yesterday.

1956

THE DERRY JOURNAL, MONDAY, 24th DECEMBER, 1956.

Girls from the Nazareth House, Derry, spent an enjoyable time at the annual Christmas treat provided for them by the Rialto Cinema. Mr. F. Hyland, manager of the cinema, is seen presenting gifts to his little guests.

THE DERRY JOURNAL FRIDAY, 7th JUNE, 1957

Boys from St. Joseph's, Termonbacca, photographed before leaving Derry on a tour of Inishowen. The outing — the first of what is hoped will be an annual affair -- was organised by the Social Committee of the B.S.R. factory. Social Committee representatives at rear of photo are Messrs. Thomas Kyle, Patrick Walsh, Philip Walsh and Michael Doherty.

1957

A TREAT FOR THE CHILDREN

Children from the Nazareth House, Derry, were the guests at a happy Christmas party in the Rialto Cinema. Here they are seen with their host, Mr. F. J. Hyland, the manager of the cinema.

1958

THEY COMPETED IN FEIS CHORAL CLASS

Nazareth House Choir, who competed in the competition for girls' choirs (in unison) at Feis Doire Colmcille.

1958

These girls from the Nazareth House scored sweeping successes at Feis Doire Colmcille and were awarded the Bishop's Shield, awarded for the school having the highest number of aggregate points at the Feis.

1958

The Nazareth House choir, winners of the competition for girls' choirs (in unison) at Feis Doire Colmcille yesterday.

1958

1958

The St. Joseph's Amateur Boxing Club from Termonbacca now in its first full season has competed with success at tournaments throughout the county. Seen with Boxing Instructor Jimmy Loughrey (the well-known Derry flyweight) members are (from left)— Front — Jackie Simpson, Michael Ramsay, Michael Kavanagh and Patrick Simpson. Middle—Alan Brolly, Brendan Devlin, Eugene Devenney, Richard Mulholland and Michael Bonner. Back—Jim Doherty, Michael Devlin, Leo Devenney, Michael McCrory, Christopher Barr, Patrick Maguire and Patrick Barr.

1959

Girls from the Nazareth House, Derry, pictured with the Bishop's Shield (awarded annually to the school whose pupils secure the highest aggregate of marks at Feis Doire Colmcille) and other trophies which they won at the Feis.

1959

1959

WORKERS GAVE TERMONBACCA BOYS A TREAT

Workers at Birmingham Sound Reproducers' Derry factory treated over sixty boys from St. Joseph's Home, Termonbacca, to a seaside outing. They went to Moville, Greencastle and Shrove. Boat trips at Moville were a feature of an enjoyable day.

GIRLS FROM NAZARETH HOUSE, BISHOP STREET

1960

The Nazareth House choir which took first place in the competition for girls' choirs (in unison) at Feis Doire Colmcille yesterday.

1961

e Holy Family choir, Nazareth House, which competed in the competition for girls' choirs (in unison) at Feis Doire Colmcille.

The Holy Family choir, Nazareth House, which competed in the competition for girls' choirs (in unison at Feis Doire Colmcille.

1961

For the first time St. Joseph's Home, Termonbacca, was represented in the Gregorian music competitions at the Feis. And they were successful. Here is the first award winning choir under Mr. Giles Doherty.

1961

THEY TOOK COVETED AWARD FOR SEVENTH TIME

Girls from the Nazareth House, Derry, who won the shield presented by Most Rev. Dr. Farren, Bishop of Derry, for the primary school whose pupils obtained the highest aggregate of points at Feis Doire Colmcille. It was the seventh time that this coveted trophy has gone to the Nazareth House.

1961

Boys from St. Joseph's Home, Termonbacca, who were the guests of the management of the A.B.C. Cinema on Christmas Eve. Photographed with the boys are the cinema manager, Mr. F. J. Hyland, and A.B.C. Minors' Club monitor Des. McFarland.

1961

Do you recognise anyone from this photograph of children from St Joseph's home for boys, Termonbacca, taken on Saturday, July 7, 1962? The kids were just about to embark on a day trip to Downings. Also included are (from left) Sr Mary Bridget, Sr Mary Annunciata and Sr Joseph Reginald.

ROUND TABLE VISITS TERMONBACCA

Members of the Derry Round Table photographed during a visit which they paid on Sunday to St. Joseph's, Termonbacca. The Round Table presented a substantial donation to St. Joseph's some months ago and were present on Sunday at the invitation of Rev. Mother Placida, Mother Superior, who is seen on the right of the picture with Dr. G. Brown, the Round Table chairman. On left is Sister Reginald and others included are F. McCraney (vice-chairman of the Round Table), R. G. Hamilton (hon. treasurer), Dr. E. E. Spence, A. W. Jack, LL.B., Dr. H. Lindsay, Dr. H. Leitch, D. Flanagan, D. Massey, C. Smith, A. McIlrath, D. Galbraith, some of the boys from St. Joseph's and F. G. Guckian and J. Melaugh, of the Termonbacca Aid Association.

1962

ST. JOSEPH'S, TERMONBACCA, WHO COMPETED IN THE GREGORIAN MUSIC BOYS' CHOIRS COMPETITION AT FEIS DOIRE COLMCILLE.

1962

The author

Boys of St. Joseph's Home, Termonbacca, Derry, photographed before leaving on Saturday on their sixth annual excursion to Malin Head. The outing was arranged by the Termonbacca Visitation Committee of the Society of St. Vincent de Paul in co-operation with the Conference of the Sacred Heart, Carndonagh, where the evening tea was served. Generous gifts of confectionery, biscuits, minerals and fruit were donated by local business houses.

THE DERRY JOURNAL, FRIDAY, 3rd MAY, 1963

Girls from the Nazareth House, Derry, who won the Shield presented by Most Rev. Dr. Farren, Bishop of Derry, to the primary school whose pupils secured the highest aggregate of points at Feis Doire Colmcille. This was the ninth time that the coveted award has gone to the Nazareth House.

The awards they gained were—1st place girls' solo under 12; 1st and 2nd places girls' solo under 14; 1st place girls' solo under 16; 2nd. girls' trio under 15; 1st. violin under 10; 2nd, violin under 12; 1st, violin under 14; 1st, junior action song; 1st and 3rd in history and cup; 1st, ceili band; 1st. girls' unison choir; 2nd, girls' Gregorian and 3-part choir; children's and juvenile orchestras (cups); 1st place, double jig under 8; 3rd place, reel under 8; Gaeltacht scholarship and, of course, the Bishop's Shield.

U.S. GIFTS TO DERRY HOMES

Gifts for the children of the Nazareth House, Bishop Street, and St. Joseph's, Termonbacca, were donated at Christmas by personnel of the U.S. Navy's communications base. The gifts came from the wives at the base, the Acey-Doucey Club (First and Second Class P.O.s) and from chiefs and officers.

1963

The choir from the Nazareth House, Derry, who won the Gregorian Music competition at the Feis. They received 98 marks.

1963

Special guests at the ABC Minors' annual Christmas matinee were boys from St. Joseph's, Termonbacca, some of whom are seen being welcomed by the cinema manager, Mr. F. J. Hyland. At the matinee Mr. Hyland also handed over a cheque to the Derry Old People's Association.

THE DERRY JOURNAL FRIDAY, 30th APRIL, 1965

Girls from the Nazareth House, Derry, with the imposing list of trophies they won at Feis Doire Colmcille. Their awards were 1st, 3-part choir; 1st, Gregorian choir; 1st, open ceili band competition; 1st and 3rd, junior violin; 2nd, preparatory violin; 2nd, violin bursaries; 1st and 3rd, girls' trio; 3rd, girls' duet; cups for children's and juvenile orchestra, junior ceili band, senior action song and history; 2nd reel under 12; 3rd treble jig under 12.

In our picture on left are boys from the Nazareth House—three of them are aged four—who were runners-up, with 83 marks, in the boys' choirs (in unison) competition at Feis Doire Colmcille. CENTRE—From left, Sara Doherty, Derry, the winner, Marie Rudden, Hollybush (second) and Geraldine Grant (third) in the girls' solo competition (over 12 and under 14). RIGHT—Dancing competition prize-winners. From left—Ann Toland, Hilary Kelly, Sibal Burke, Vincent Taggart, Stella McLaughlin, Marion Given and Sylvia McLaughlin.

1965

SEASIDE OUTING FOR DERRY CHILDREN

Messrs. Jack Melaugh (left), George Allison (centre) and John Mullan (right), organisers of an annual outing for Derry children, photographed with the youngsters — they included some handicapped children and boys from St. Joseph's Home, Termonbacca—before they left for Portrush yesterday. [See "Tuesday Parade" on Page 2]

1965

THE DERRY JOURNAL, TUESDAY, 20th DECEMBER, 1966

At a Christmas party given by the staff of the Embassy Ballroom and the Melville Hotel in the Embassy for children from St. Joseph's Home, Termonbacca, the Northland Special Care School and children under the care of the city Welfare Committee.

1966

Among the little guests at the ABC Minors' annual Christmas show were these girls from the Nazareth House, Derry, and boys from St. Joseph's Home, Termonbacca. In centre of back row is Mr. F. J. Hyland, ABC cinema manager.

1966

THE DERRY JOURNAL, FRIDAY, 1st APRIL, 1966

The recently-formed Little Singers of Nazareth, with Mick McWilliams, who have made successful appearances at concerts in Belfast, Portstewart, Desertmartin and in St. Columb's Hall, Derry.

1966

Christmas presents were donated by the Go Go Social Club, Derry, to the Nazareth House, St. Joseph's Home, Termonbacca and St. Columb's Hospital. This picture was taken when the gifts were presented to Termonbacca. Santa Claus is Mr. Jim McCloskey.

THE DERRY JOURNAL, FRIDAY, 16th JUNE, 1967

1967

"OPPORTUNITY KNOCKS" FOR NAZARETH HOUSE CEILIDH BAND

Tomorrow night this ceilidh band from Nazareth House, Bishop Street, Derry, will be appearing on the A.T.V. Hughie Green programme, "Opportunity Knocks." Photographed with the children is Sister M. Aidan, who is in charge of the band. Front (from left)—Mary McCrystal, Jeanette McCloskey, Margaret Chambers, and Bernadette Coyle. Back row—Celine O'Callaghan, Kathleen Ward, Ann Simpson, Marie Tierney and Eileen Brogan.

The band have also an engagement with the Eamonn Andrews Studio on 28th June, and will be appearing in a film later this year.

When Mr. James MacCafferty in 1956 took the Little Gaelic Singers to the U.S.A. for the first time, children of the Nazareth House (who comprised two-thirds of the group) played their own Irish dancing accompaniment, and these violinists were the nucleus of the ceilidhe band formed a few years later. The band has won many trophies at local feis-eanna.

Tony Black, Giles Doherty, Frank McLaughlin and Breandan de Glin have given their services as teachers, and musical arrangements were done by Redmond Friel and James MacCafferty.

The programme will be introduced by Sister Aidan, who will travel with the children to Manchester for the occasion.

1967

THE DERRY JOURNAL, FRIDAY, 14th APRIL, 1967

Children from the Nazareth House, Derry, won eight cups and other awards, including the Bishop's Shield (awarded annually to the primary school whose pupils secure the highest number of points) at Feis Doire Colmcille. Their successes included—first place in three-part choir, Gregorian choir, unison choir, junior action song and girls' trio (under 18); 1st and 3rd in the girls' trio (under 16); 2nd in girls' duet (under 16); 1st in boys' solo (under 8); 3rd in violin solo (under 10); 1st and 2nd in violin solo (under 12); 1st in violin solo (under 14), violin solo (under 16) and violin solo (under 16); cup winners for children's orchestra, juvenile orchestra, junior ceili band and senior ceili band.

1967

Due to the generosity of two Derrymen, as well as that of the patrons of the Johnny Quigley Lounge Bar and the Red Lion Bar, plus donations from C.P.O.'s Mess, H.M.S. Stalker, 45 children from Derry had a marvellous day at Portrush yesterday. Thirty-five of the children were from Termonbacca and the remainder from the Derry Polio Association. The two men behind the outing as they have been for the past number of years, are Mr. John Melaugh, R.N., and Mr. George Allison, of the City Hotel. Every year they save the commission they receive from the Derry City "Daily Draw" and pool it in the summer so that some children can have a day at the seaside.

Nazareth House Ceili Band delighted English and Belgian audiences

DERRY'S Nazareth House Ceili Band returned home this week from a very successful tour of the English Midlands. They went over at the invitation of the Derry Association of Corby, Northants, and they were given a great welcome in every venue they played. They were invited to return again in the near future.

The Mayor of Corby, Mr. Moon, presented each member of the band with a replica of the city coat of arms at a civic reception. At the reception the Mayor praised the group on their fine performances during the tour.

A few days before their English tour the Nazareth House Ceili Band had just returned from Belgium, where they were also given a great welcome. The Derry band had the honour of representing Ireland at 13th International Festival of Jambes, Namur. The audiences really appreciated the traditional music played by the group.

"Tres enchantant" were the words on the lips of the audience. Once more the Derry ambassadors of Irish music and dancing were given a civic reception, at which they were presented with copper plates bearing the Jambes coat of arms. The band received a standing ovation from the big audience at the final concert.

The director of the festival, M. Mosseray, said of the band's performance: "They literally stole the show." Other participants in the festival from Italy, Belgium, France, Sweden, Spain and the Ukraine, also expressed this sentiment. The Ukrainians showed their appreciation of the young Derry musicians by warmly embracing the children.

Accompanying the band on both tours was a pupil of the De Glin Colmcille Irish Dancing Academy, Elaine Eaton, who was a very successful soloist with the band.

1972

Work at the extension to St. Joseph's, Termonbacca, is nearing completion.

Tomorrow a Flag Day is being held by the Termonbacca Aid Association and the annual house-to-house envelope collection will be taken up this week-end.

The Association once again appeals to the generosity of the people of Derry to help the children and Sisters of Nazareth in Termonbacca.

"A considerable sum is still needed to complete the new building presently under construction, and during the past year it has been impossible to carry out normal fund raising activities," they say. "Realising the extreme needs of these under-privileged children we feel certain that we do not appeal in vain."

1972

Over six hundred children from seventeen schools took part in the fourth annual Termonbacca Aid Association schools' charity walk.

Proceeds of the walk this year will be shared between St. Joseph's Home, Termonbacca, and the Special Care School, Northland Road, for the provision of a physical activity and recreational centre for the handicapped.

Two cheques, each for £500, were handed over to the two charities during the week at Termonbacca.

Our picture shows Sister Hilary, on behalf of Rev. Mother Colm, Termonbacca, receiving one cheque and Mr. James R. Doherty, chairman of the Parents' Association, and Mr. Charlie Herron, principal, receiving the other on behalf of the Special Care School. Also in the picture are representatives of the various schools which took part.

At the presentation both Sister Hilary and Mr. Doherty thanked the children, their teacher and parents for their magnificent effort.

1975

Group pictured at St. Joseph's Home, Termonbacca, Derry when first aid certificates were presented to Sisters and children in the Home by Capt. George White, G.M. Courses in first aid were conducted in the Home by Lt. Joseph O'Kane and Cpl. Manus Shields, of the Derry Order of Malta.

Seated centre, *(from left)*, are Sister Domingo, Lt. O'Kane, Captain White, , Rev. Mother Colm, Vol. Cecilia Carlin, Cpl. Shiels and Sister Pontianus.

Back row *(from left)* Sister Theresa, Brigid McCrossan, John McCrossan, Kevin Carty, Sister Laurence, Helen Green, Sister Michael, Jerry Goodman, Daniel McCrossan, Damlen. McKenna and Sister Hililary.

Seated in from *(from left)* Bernard McEldowney, Gerard McGoldrick, PaddyJoe Quigley, William Lynch, Eugene Gallagher, Stephen McConnagh and Joseph McGavigan.

Children from St. Joseph's, Termonbacca, and Nazareth House, Bishop St., Derry, pictured before leaving on an outing to Shrove and Ballyliffin. The trip was organised by O.N.D. (business studies) 1st year students at Derry College of Technology as part of their community work for the liberal studies course. The money was raised by the students by car-washing.

Nazareth House P.S., winners of the McCloskey Plaque award for the group dramatisation (open) competition

Tributes were paid to Sister Teresa a popular member of the Sisters of Nazareth Community at St Josephs Home Termonbacca, Derry, at a function held in the Home. When she was the recipient of presentations of a silver salver and scroll from the old boys of Termonbacca. Sister Teresa who is a native of Limerik has spent the past seventeen years at St Josephs caring for the children. Sister Teresa has been transferred to Nazareth House Birmingham England and she left Derry yesterday to take up her new appointment.

1978

Joseph McGavican is pictured making the presentation on behalf of the Old Boys.

Group pictured at the Athletic F.C. annual presentation of trophies at St. Joseph's, Termonbacca. Seated centre second row are, Mr. Lawrence Hasson, president and Mr. Jim O'Hea, club leader.

Workers on the farm Termonbacca - 1978

Termonbacca Football Team - 1979
Left to right: Nathan Quigley, John Paul Henry, Michael Goodman, Alan Killen, Gerd McGlone, Lawrence Hamilton, Gerry Goodman, Joe Kelly

Derry Journal

3rd MARCH, 1992 — 56 PAGES — Established 1772 — PRICE: 35p — (Republic of Ireland). 40

His Eminence, Cardinal Cahal Daly, who presided at the Centenary Mass of Thanksgiving, in Nazareth House, Derry, seated in centre with Most. Rev. Dr. Edward Daly, who was the Celebrant. Also seated are, from left, Mother Aidan, Regional Superior, Sister Annunciata, Superior, Nazareth House, Mother Bernard Mary, Mother General, Sisters of Nazareth, Hammersmith, London and the Mayor, Councillor Mary Bradley. Standing, from left, Rev. Bernard J. Canon Canning, author of the booklet, "The Poor Sisters of Nazareth and Derry", Mr. John Hume M.P., M.E.P., Mgr. Martin Rooney P.P., V.F., Most Rev. Dr. Seamus Hegarty, Bishop of Raphoe, Most Rev. Francis Lagan, Auxiliary Bishop of Derry, Rt Rev. James McGuinness Bishop of Nottingham, Mgr Austin Duffy P.P., V.G. and Mr. Liam Bradley. (3/3/A34 (see centre pages)

Sisters of Nazareth

A century of service

EXACTLY one hundred years ago the then Bishop of Derry, Most Reverend John Keys O'Doherty, invited the Sisters of Nazareth to establish a home in Derry to care for the elderly and needy children.

Mother Mary of the Nativity and six Sisters established the first foundation of the Sisters of Nazareth in the Derry diocese on March 2, 1892, in 'Sunnyside,' the original name of their House in Bishop Street.

In the coming months there will be a variety of activities to celebrate the one hundredth anniversary and the present Community hopes that everyone associated with Nazareth House will take part at some stage.

Recently, the Sisters were accorded a Civic Reception in the Guildhall at which the Mayor, Councillor Mary Bradley, praised the work carried out by the Sisters in the city and said the local community owed them a great deal.

On Sunday, March 1, a Centenary Mass of Thanksgiving will be celebrated in Nazareth House Chapel at which the Principal Celebrant will be Most Reverend Edward Daly, Bishop of Derry. Joining him will be Most Reverend Francis Lagan, Auxiliary Bishop of Derry; Most Reverend James McGuinness, Bishop of Nottingham, a native of Derry; and priests, religious and friends from all over the diocese.

His Eminence, Cathal Cardinal Daly, Archbishop of Armagh and Primate of All-Ireland, will preside at the Mass of Thanksgiving.

Dates will be announced later for the open day for benefactors; the 'Old Girls' reunion day; and the celebrations for the present residents and staff.

Speaking on behalf of the present Community, Nazareth House, the Superior, Sister Mary Annunciata, said: "We take this opportunity to publicly thank the people of Derry for their most generous support and loyalty to the House over the last one hundred years. Its success is truly a tribute to the people of this city. We pray that God will bless each one of them."

NAZARETH HOUSE, BLACKBURN

CHILDREN, NAZARETH HOUSE, BLACKBURN

NAZARETH HOUSE, SOUTHAMPTON

JUNIOR BOYS, SOUTHAMPTON

NAZARETH HOUSE, OXFORD

CHILDREN, NAZARETH HOUSE, BLACKBURN

NAZARETH HOUSE, MIDDLESBOROUGH

NAZARETH HOUSE, NEWCASTLE-ON-TYNE

THE OLD PEOPLE, NAZARETH HOUSE, HAMMERSMITH

THE CHAPEL NAZARETH HOUSE, HAMMERSMITH

SISTERS' CHOIR NAZARETH HOUSE, HAMMERSMITH

OLD LADIES, NAZARETH HOUSE, EAST FINCHLEY

SOUTHEND BABY BOYS' BAND

NAZARETH HOUSE, EAST FINCHLEY, LONDON

NAZARETH HOUSE, SOUTHEND

GIRLS, NAZARETH HOUSE, SOUTHSEA

NAZARETH BOYS, WESTBURY-ON-TRYM

NAZARETH HOUSE, BEXHILL

BOYS AT DRILL, NAZARETH HOUSE, KIMBERLEY

NAZARETH HOUSE, CARDIFF

BOYS, NAZARETH HOUSE, SWANSEA

NAZARETH HOUSE, BRISBANE

GIRLS AT DRILL, ABERDEEN

NAZARETH HOUSE, KILMARNOCK

TWENTY-FIVE GIRLS WHO EMIGRATED TO BRISBANE, 1926

NAZARETH HOUSE, BALLARAT, AUSTRALIA

NATIVE CHILDREN, NAZARETH FARM, FOURTEEN STREAMS.

BAND BOYS, NAZARETH HOUSE, JOHANNESBERG, S.AFRICA

REUNION OF OLD BOYS, BALLARAT, AUSTRALIA

NATIVE CHILDREN, FOURTEEN STREAMS, S. AFRICA

NAZARETH HOUSE, CHRISTCHURCH, N.ZEALAND

NAZARETH HOUSE, BALLARAT

RE-UNION OF BOYS AND GIRLS, SEBASTOPOL.

NAZARETH HOUSE, JOHANNESBERG

HERE I AM IN THE POTTERIES
MARATHON 1991

MY WIFE, ONE OF OUR DAUGHTERS AND FRIENDS AT A CELEBRATION,
1991

MYSELF HOLDING THE 100 MARATHON CUP,
BEFORE A PRESENTATION

JUST A HANDFULL OF OUR MEMBERS GETTING TOGETHER
BEFORE THE AMSTERDAM MARATHON

BEING INTERVIEWED IN THE LONDON MARATHON 1992

ME AND FELLOW RUNNERS IN COSTUME AT THE FINISH
OF THE LONDON MARATHON 1992

162 MARATHON ACHIEVEMENTS

During my time marathon running I was very proud to complete 100 full marathons, and also became the first man from Derry, Northern Ireland to accomplish this.

My best time from my marathons was running 26 miles and 365 yds. in the official time of 2 hours, 50 minutes and 3 seconds.

I went on to complete 162 full marathons of which 22 of these races were run for various charities. I carried a pair of double aluminium 11ft. ladders on my shoulders, and hence on the marathon circuit I am known as *'THE LADDER MAN'*.

In all I have collected around £40,000 for charities. I even took my ladders to the Stockholm Marathon and Norway Marathon. I completed the Belfast Marathon in 3 hours and 9 minutes. Unfortunately I did not get my pint of Guiness at the finish line as promised, so they still owe me a pint.

The best and most exciting marathon of all was The Washington Corps Marathon in the U.S.A.

My best supporter in all of my marathons has been my wife Barbara. She was always there at the finish line cheering me home.